TRUDEAU

PIERRE ELLIOTT TRUDEAU   JOHN TURNER

JEAN CHRÉTIEN   LESTER B. PEARSON

GEORGE ELLIOTT

Trude

Long March & Shining Path

GASPEREAU PRESS LIMITED ¶ PRINTERS & PUBLISHERS

Beati Anni Decimi MMVII

CLARKE

au

À Son Excellence
la très honorable
Michaëlle Jean,
Gouverneur général
du Canada

&

Geraldine Elizabeth Clarke
(1939–2000)
&
Lillian Liu Jackson
(1937–95)
Two Teachers

&

William Lloyd Clarke
(1935–2005)
Artist

it is better to be a part of beauty
for one instant and then cease to
exist than to exist forever
and never be a part of beauty
MARQUIS

Und jene, die schön sind, o wer hält sie zurück?
RILKE, DIE ZWEITE ELEGIE

A wise nation … decorates the tombs
of its illustrious dead …
JOSEPH HOWE

CONTENTS

ATTENTION!

Beauty is difficult ...
POUND, CANTO LXXIV

This literary work offers an interpretation of the lives of several historical personages, all rendered fictitiously. The author has distorted known facts, altered dates, imagined dialogues, and invented situations. His characters should not be confused with actual individuals, either living or dead. This dramatic poem is purely a theatre of imagination.

AU LECTEUR

Damn each history! Each bio!
There can be but the one "Trudeau."
But *your* Trudeau? And *my* Trudeau?[1]
On doit chercher l'homme dans ses mots.

Each portrait's *une belle infidèle*:
Blame the artist? Blame the model?
Perspective veers, look after look:
Both film and play betray the book.

Rhyme's, too, *déja vu*—medieval—
Even in octosyllable
Doubled as couplet (so I hear)—
Art as *avant-garde* as Chaucer.

But Trudeau—*ours*—opposed, through verse,
Posed versions of our universe.

---

1   Cf. Pound, Canto II

VRAI:
UN ESSAI

*Our heroes and their narratives are an
index to our character and conception
of our role in the universe.*
SLOTKIN[2]

During my 'Africadian', crypto-socialist, poetry-impassioned
youth, my heroes were warrior-intellectuals—scarved, lone figures.
I romanticized such chivalric characters as the speaker in Conrad
Kent Rivers' vivid poem, "Four sheets to the wind (and a one way
ticket to France)" (1962):

*As a child
I bought a red scarf and women told me how beautiful it looked,
wandering through the sous-sols as France wandered through me.*

I yearned to live like that—in gorgeous exile, to sport a scarf and
a beret and wander night-steeped avenues. I admired solitary
Romantics. Thus, as a tyro poet, I chose, as my models, dashing,
difficult artists and politicians: *avant-garde* reactionary Ezra Pound;
dictator-philosopher Mao Zedong; free-speech poet Irving Layton;
jazz trumpeter Miles Davis; pop bard Bob Dylan; orator Malcolm
X; and The Right Honourable Pierre Elliott Trudeau.

True: the scrupulosity of biographers and historians reveals,
steadily, the atrocious failings of the members of this suspect
septet. My idols were, perhaps mainly, dastards. But they were also,
for me, inescapable.

My pantheon honours the 1960s, but it cannot be helped: I was
born in 1960, and grew up with the recordings and the books of
these men in my home. Thus, I have written poetry about them all,

---

2 See Slotkin (564).

and my poetics is informed by their styles and texts. These artist-politicos and politico-artists radiated, it seemed to me, insouciant sassiness as well as tragicomic charisma.

Pointedly, Trudeau was one of only two Canadians to 'place' in my catalogue of robust intellectuals and artists. Now here he is—the star of this show.[3]

Admittedly, my decision to write up Trudeau—to actually put my words in his mouth—is peculiar: I am neither a Liberal nor a liberal. (I am, quixotically, a 'Baptist Marxist'.) However, as a 'visible minority' person (my official identity in white-majority Canada), I seize the right to "write what I like" (to cite Steve Biko), including this libretto about a wealthy, European male; one canonized—and demonized—by hordes of white Canuck lawyers and social scientists, but also by poets, artists, journalists, and historians.

Trudeau was, is, though, a cult figure for many Canadians *de couleur*. To only mention Anglo-Afro-'Cano' writers who place him in their texts, I must cite Austin Clarke, Max Dorsinville, Suzette Mayr, Andrew Moodie, Hazelle Palmer, and Oscar Peterson.[4] Considerations of Trudeau by 'Third World' Canadians are absent, however, from media celebrations or interrogations of the man and his legacy. In line with the precept that Canada is a white country, 'multicultural' Canadians are expected to limit their political expression to raucous, ghettoized, candidate-nomination meetings. Yet, our vision of Trudeau would be enhanced were we to appreciate that he really was *un citoyen du monde*, the first prime minister who was comfortable with a Canada that looked more like

---

3 I never met Trudeau, but I did see him, up close, once. On a Grade 9 class trip to Ottawa, the "National Capital," in June 1975, my pre-high-school classmates and I stopped outside 24 Sussex Drive, the Prime Minister's Residence, just in time to see a black sedan emerge and, temporarily, block the sidewalk. Then the passenger-side rear window slid down, and Trudeau stuck his head into the bright, late spring sunlight to ask us how we were enjoying Ottawa. We answered in a singsong chorus, chirruping the usual tourist positives. He nodded affably, smiled, waved, and the sedan purred into the future. (Now follows the non sequitur: Two weeks later, I began to write songs—the anticipation of poetry.)

4 For the record, may I say I espy Trudeauvian qualities in my late motorcycle-riding, poetry-reading, land-and-seascape-painting, gal-serenading, and social-working father?

Expo 67 and less like the Grand Ole Opry. He was, in short, a *pur-et-dur* internationalist.

Recall that Trudeau was the only Liberal Party leadership candidate to mention the assassination of Martin Luther King, Jr., the previous night, in his April 5, 1968, address to delegates. (His campaign poster—a groovy silhouette—mirrored iconic images of the just-slain, Latin American guerilla leader Che Guevara.) His writings—see *Deux innocents en Chine rouge* (1961)—display familiarity with classical Chinese philosophy and contemporary Chinese politics. (Note, too, that *The Essential Trudeau* [1998] recycles the style of Mao's "little red book.") Trudeau met Mao Zedong twice—in 1960 and in 1973—and his signal campaign promise in 1968 was to restore diplomatic relations with China (accomplished in 1970). In 1976, he riled some Canadians by touring Cuba and shouting, "Viva Castro!" Eventually, Trudeau visited liberated South Africa and hoisted a beer at a *shebeen*.[5] He loved donning the garb of other cultures: a turban here, a robe there. No Canadian prime minister before or since has associated as closely with the Third World—or with Canadians 'of colour.'[6]

Yet, this libretto crafts no elegy. In his youth, Trudeau flirted with fascistic nativism, even dreaming of leading an army to create an independent state—one French, Catholic, and homogeneous. While he later repudiated, demonstrably, this regressive politics, I believe he continued to harbour—despite his pacifist rhetoric and gestures—a fascination with armed force and strong men. In this regard, he was like many other artists and intellectuals who craved power—or who wielded it: Mao, Marinetti, Mussolini, Mishima. However, knowledge of the Holocaust likely shifted Trudeau from his original conservative and authoritarian leanings. I imagine that his revulsion at this unspeakable acme of blood-and-soil racism—extermination, genocide—compelled him to liberalism,

---

5 A South African township tavern.
6 One endearing aspect of Trudeau was his penchant for the phrase "the Canadian people." Though a bland and unexceptional concept, it remains eclectically rare in Canadian political discourse. (Our leaders prefer to speak of 'Canadians' or 'the people of Canada.') Trudeau's radical rhetoric *pretended* that Canadians really were one people, denying our local-colour fealties.

federalism, multiculturalism, a staunch defence of minorities, and a mild socialism. I also expect Trudeau secreted guilt for not having enlisted to combat militarized racism during the Anti-Fascist War. Perhaps he found expiation by becoming a fierce cosmopolitan, insisting on the essential equality of human experience by voyaging, endlessly, tirelessly, and (often in the style of a guerilla) alone, into the wilderness—natural, urban, or political.

Arguably, study and travel transformed the erstwhile provincial fascist into a cosmo, anti-nationalist liberal. Certainly, this identity was the one he espoused when he entered national public life in the 20th century's most vital post-World War II decade, the 1960s, and then became prime minister in its most crucial year, 1968.[7] Strangely, while the streets of Paris, Washington, Beijing, Mexico City, and Prague blazed, that year, with riot, resistance, and protest, Canadian streets resounded with the carnival of "Trudeaumania."[8] How typical of Canada—this Yankee monarchy: Rather than struggle for an actual revolution in 1968, Canadians—even many

---

7　Trudeau's political life negotiated the two defining discourses of the post-WWII era: the Cold War (or East-West rivalry) and decolonization (or North-South conflict). In terms of the Cold War, Trudeau was a peacenik, presiding over the re-orientation of the Canadian Army from 'defence' to 'peacekeeping' and, despite his animus for brutally enforced Communist conformity, reaching out to Soviet Bloc states and China. He continued his usual contradictions, however, right to the end of his premiership, touring the globe in 1983 to protest a renewed U.S. and U.S.S.R. arms build-up, yet also approving U.S. testing of cruise missiles in Canada. Addressing decolonization movements, Trudeau understood, far better than his critics, that Canada was, in the 1960s and '70s, facing the anomaly of *three* simultaneous struggles: 1) the effervescent (not 'quiet') effort of Francophone-majority Québec to displace Anglo capital and professional control with its own homegrown entrepreneurs and bureaucrats; 2) the aspirations of English Canadians to redefine themselves as less stodgily British, more jazzily American, while attempting to reduce U.S. cultural and economic influence; and 3) the cultural and political transformation of 'Indians, Eskimos, and Half-Breeds' into First Nations peoples / Aboriginals, Inuit, and Métis. (Feminist insurgency wrought additional progress.) Any one of these processes could have moved, in classic anti-colonial fashion, from loud reformism to bloody revolution (and some groups, notably the Front de Libération du Québec, did make the effort). From the standpoint of a revolutionary theorist like Frantz Fanon, Trudeau was just another *comprador*, one of those bourgeois leaders "violent in their words and reformist in their attitudes" (59). "Non-violence," warns Fanon, "is an attempt to settle the colonial problem around a green baize table ..." (61). (U.S. Historian Theodore H. White informs us that "All great political struggles ... are underlain by a struggle of cultures ..." [331].) Nevertheless, it

Québécois—simply voted for Trudeau, an 'iron man,' but one with a flower in his lapel and a girl on each arm.

One reason for his success, especially in 1968,[9] is that Trudeau answered Canada's yearning for a John F. Kennedy all its own, a 'star' who could combine intellectual sparkle, physical vigour, elite privilege, and 'sex appeal,' and look terrific on television. Like J.F.K, P.E.T. delivered, vicariously, the revitalizing feeling of "the supercharged oxygen of life hurtling through one's veins" (Lubin 139).[10] Kennedy preserved that cultural currency—of jaunty masculinity—because he perished young. Although Trudeau lived to be an octogenarian, he maintained an aura of iconic, zesty, and dangerous youth.

I base my story on Trudeau's writings—as well as on his *Memoirs* (1993), that defensively confessional and graphically chatty book. His political autobiography leaves out, naturally, many of his grotesque (and revealing) *faux pas*, including, in 1970, his government's plan to assimilate First Nations peoples. Trudeau

---

is either to Trudeau's credit or discredit (depending on one's ideological position) that his insight into both rightist and leftist decolonization models allowed his government to prod Canada's popular movements along peaceful, democratic paths. His 'rational' answer to passionate and utopian radical sentiment was constitutionalism—its absolute antithesis. Then again, as much as Fanon and Trudeau may be positioned as dreadful foes, the former's precept that nationalist parties erect, eventually, "an authentic ethnic dictatorship" (183), verifies Trudeau's unflinching critique of this extremism. But when Fanon commands, "We must not voodoo the people, nor dissolve them in emotion and confusion" (200), he could be sampling one of Trudeau's *Cité libre* denunciations of nationalist fever.

8   Montréal 'hosted' a Québec nationalist riot one night in June 1968. But "Trudeaumania" still trumped secessionist rock-throwing.

9   1968 was the 1848 of the 20th century: a year of failed, libertarian revolt.

10 According to David M. Lubin, Kennedy came to represent "liberal democratic capitalism guided by aristocratic leadership with high ideals and a common touch" (284). Surely this was Trudeau's *meaning*, though he Canadianized it by emphasizing an intellectual *noblesse oblige* and preferring aloofness to love-ins. William L. Van Deburg insists, "No single individual manifested the essence of the modern culture hero in more compelling fashion than John F. Kennedy" (6), thanks to his "scene-stealing charisma" (245). For Canadians, Trudeau enacted this scintillating symbolism. (No one should ignore, either, the spillover effect, upon Trudeau's own electoral appeal, of American mania for the messianic, presidential ambitions of New York Senator Robert F. Kennedy—J.F.K.'s doomed brother—that charmed and bloody spring of 1968.)

also ignores his own callous dismissal of the agonies of Biafra in 1970 and of Poland in 1980. Such pregnant omissions signal that, while Trudeau's rhetoric was provocative, his practice was conservative. To apply a Maoist formula, he was 'left in form but right in essence.'[11]

Eschewing sociology, political science, economics, and constitutional law, this libretto avoids definitive realism. It is a paean to the liberationist mood of 1968: Prague's "Spring," Paris's "May," and Canada's "Tory" version—namely, "Trudeaumania." Yet, my Trudeau is not the now-deceased immortal, but rather the Warhol silkscreen; not surreal, but sidereal: an insubordinate reality, half-Plato, half-Chaplin. *My* Trudeau is *the* slapstick contrarian—with Pound's *brio*, Mao's ascetic aesthetic, Layton's macho assertiveness, Davis's sunglasses, X's sass, and Dylan's alluring mystery.

GEORGE ELLIOTT CLARKE
Toronto, Ontario
Nisan VII

---

11 Cf. Karnow (240).

Biko, Steve. *I Write What I Like: A selection of his writings.* Ed. Aelred Stubbs. C.R. 1978. London: Heinemann, 1979.

Fanon, Frantz. *The Wretched of the Earth.* New York: Grove Press, 1968. Trans. Constance Farrington. *Les damnés de la terre.* Paris: François Maspero, 1961.

Karnow, Stanley. *Mao and China: Inside China's Cultural Revolution.* 1972. New York: Viking Penguin, 1984.

Lubin, David M. *Shooting Kennedy: JFK and the Culture of Images.* Berkeley: University of California Press, 2003.

Rivers, Conrad Kent. "Four sheets to the wind (and a one way ticket to France)." 1962. *The still voice of Harlem.* London: Paul Bremen, 1972. 18.

Slotkin, Richard. *Regeneration Through Violence: The Mythology of the American Frontier, 1600–1860.* Middleton, CT: Wesleyan University Press, 1973.

Trudeau, Pierre Elliott. *Deux innocents en Chine rouge.* With Jacques Hébert. Montréal: Les Éditions de l'homme, 1961.

_____. *The Essential Trudeau.* Ed. Ron Graham. Toronto: McClelland & Stewart, 1998.

_____. *Memoirs.* Toronto: McClelland & Stewart, 1993.

Van Deburg, William L. *Black Camelot: African-American Culture Heroes in Their Times, 1960–1980.* Chicago: University of Chicago Press, 1997.

White, Theodore H. *Breach of Faith: The Fall of Richard Nixon.* New York: Atheneum Publishers & Reader's Digest Press, 1975.

DRAMATIS PERSONAE

Beauty will have to describe
itself from now on.
FINDLEY

Ranked in order of appearance.
Players are not bound by their descriptions.

Mao Zedong
Chairman of the Communist Party of China
This baritone may also play Fidel Castro and Jacques Fanon.
He may be Chinese or Cuban or Québécois. If he also plays
John F. Kennedy, he may also be Catholic.

Pierre Elliott Trudeau
Adventurer, Writer, Prime Minister of Canada
This tenor may be an Aboriginal / First Nations (or Métis) person.

Yu Xuanji
A Chinese poetess
This soprano may double as Simone Cixous. She may be
Montagnaise, a Mauricienne, or a Monégasque.

John F. Kennedy
Senator of Massachusetts

Fidel Castro
President of Cuba

Lt. Neruda
An Afro-Cuban aide to Castro
This jazz/soul vocalist may also play
Roscoe Robertson and Nelson Mandela.

Simone Cixous
A Québécoise journalist

Roscoe Robertson
An African-Canadian jazz pianist

Margaret
A Liberal and a liberal
This singer should be Indian (out of Kashmir or Bihar) with a
command of Indian vocal/musical traditions. Or she could be
Italian. Let her identity be as indeterminate as Canadian actress
Rae Dawn Chong in Jean-Jacques Annaud's film Quest for Fire
(1981) or Spanish actress Rosa Maria Almirall (Lina Romay) in
Jesus Franco's film El misterio del castillo rojo *(1972).*

Jacques Fanon
A Québécois liberationist

Nelson Mandela
President of South Africa

Vistas
Revolutionary China
Revolutionary Cuba
French-Colonial Tahiti
Democratic South Africa
Quiet Revolution Québec
'Cool' and 'Mod' Canada

ACT I

Elegance is refusal.
COCO CHANEL

Scene i: Nanjing, China, April 1949

Sound of machine-gun fire and explosions. Civil war! The People's Liberation Army is capturing Nanjing. Enter Mao Zedong, aged 56, in a military coat and a red-star-emblazoned cap. He carries a pistol at his side and a satchel on his back. He bears a red flag in one hand. With a flourish, he plants the flag in a cleft between two rocks. He takes a pen and paper from the bag, sits on a rock amid an alpine meadow, and begins to write.

MAO: Seizing the mountain, this crazy,
    Jagged zigzag of crags, hazy
    With wind-raised snow, I see rocks ply
    Toward the moon's white gravity,
    Imagine dragons' wings brushing
    My head, while my soldiers, pushing
    To the stars, make the weak sky break,
    Topple bosses and thieves, and take
    History into our own hands—
    Blood-baptized, scarlet, crimson hands.
      Now freed, China unscrolls, awaits
    Red calligraphy, our dictates—
    Brush-stroke or sword-stroke. Snow, weightless,
    Hammers earth with sparkling softness:
      This world is mutable: mountains
    Melt to coral reefs and fountains.

The People's Liberation—Sing!
Our Army has captured Nanjing.

Mao sets down his pen and paper and withdraws his pistol.
Statuesquely, he dances with it and aims it at the moon.

A ballad unfurls, line by line:
We mow down traitors, nine by nine.
Bugles bawl, our machine guns hiss;
Landlords fall; blood—theirs—stinks like piss.

Up, soldiers! Kill! Scatter foes like colts!
Slay with the shock of thunderbolts!

Political power flows and runs
Out of the barrels of the People's guns.

Starving babes howl: that's why we war:
Meat's more filling than metaphor.
Bread tastes sweeter than honeyed gold!
Our wealth is loot that bankers hold.

Preach like persuasive Marxist-Leninists—
Stuff fat bellies with bullets for breakfasts,
Bullets for banquets, bullets for cocktails.
Crush greasy gizzards! Spill slimy entrails!

Pit *we* against *they*!
Massacre all parasites!
Sink em in the sea!
Tommy-gun em into pits!

The People's Liberation—Sing!
Our Army has captured Nanjing.

Mao continues to prance and brandish his pistol. However, sounds
of machine-gun fire and explosions are now half-muffled by fog.
Out of this mist strides Pierre Elliott Trudeau, 29, with a long
beard and a backpack, wearing a fashionable cashmere coat, a

scarf, and a beret. He stands across the stage from Mao. Each man is oblivious to the other.

TRUDEAU: How can men fire guns at others?
    In such fog, aren't all men brothers?
    Who is fighting whom? Why? What for?
    In history's fog and fog of war?

    During Hitler's war, I did what I liked—
    Loafed in Quebec and motorbiked,
    So proud, with a Prussian helmet on,
    A preppy lad, crying *"Révolution!"*

    I felt embarrassed, damned, and lost
    To spy the X-rays of Holocaust—
    The ovens and bones of Auschwitz—
    While I lounged in swank ski chalets.

    To exorcise that war I missed,
    I tour a globe ruddy in gist.
    Across this world's blood-soaked atlas,
    History cuts men into grass.

    In 1948, I saw
    The birth of Israel, that awe,
    Emerge from genocide and stand
    Embattled in the desert sand.

    Now in China, I shadow Mao—
    His Long March through civil war.
    Crossing river and mountain pass,
    I slip my race, eclipse my class.

    How can men fire guns at others?
    In such fog, aren't all men brothers?
    Who fights whom? And why? What for?
    In history's fog and fog of war?

Mao adds his smoky commentary.

MAO: Political power flows and runs
   Out of the barrels of our guns.

Still encased in fog, Trudeau speaks while setting down his backpack.

TRUDEAU: Pining for Papa, perished young,
   I need to prove I'm more than strong:
   Athletic, peripatetic,
   A suave, sensual ascetic …

   But is all I am sheer mint in Montreal?
   May I tear off skin and ebb ethereal?

   Crossing river and mountain pass,
   I jettison my race and class.
   I wander, drift, to test myself,
   And, against brute fate, wield my fist.

Trudeau shakes his fist. But then he kneels.

TRUDEAU: *Papa, sans toi, j'ai perdu le soleil:*
   Sans ton amour, le monde est un deuil.

   Papa, without you, I've lost the sun:
   Without your love, your laughter, I'm alone.

Mist melts. Brandishing his pistol, Mao accosts the now-standing Trudeau.

MAO: Tell who you are before I fire!

TRUDEAU: I'm a student from the Sorbonne.

MAO: Why's a foreigner at a civil war?

TRUDEAU: Travel is my dissertation.
   India I've viewed, now China—
   Marxist *deus ex machina*.

MAO: Are you Capitalist or Communist?

TRUDEAU: [*Shrugging.*] Truthfully, I'm just a canoeist.

MAO: Whose side are you on?

TRUDEAU: This mountainside we're on.

MAO: What are you doing in Nanjing?

TRUDEAU: To witness your triumph, Mao Zedong,
   And eye the future, while it's young—
   China's slippage from Europe's gang.

MAO: Yes, I am he, General Mao:
   Poet who pries peasant from plough.
   Who are you?

TRUDEAU: Pierre Elliott Trudeau,
   Montreal-born, now reading law.

Mao shakes hands with Trudeau, then slaps his back.

MAO: English-snarling thugs with big bucks
   Mash up all you pea-soup Canucks.
   Quebec plays Canada's Hong Kong.

TRUDEAU: General Mao, you're wise, but wrong:
   Quebec fields a democracy.

MAO: Not so. Check Maurice Duplessis!

TRUDEAU: Never confuse the people with their king.

MAO: Retire their tyrant, and the people sing!

TRUDEAU: [*Shrugging.*] Your politics pushes war, war—
　　Tireless, ceaseless, never-ending war.

MAO: Capitalists bid workers starve:
　　Poor folk are meat that rich folk carve.

TRUDEAU: And so revolution must befall?

MAO: Backward things are identical:
　　If you don't hit them, they won't fall.

TRUDEAU: But I'm free, sole, a liberal!

MAO: Liberalism touts claptrap
　　And quibbles and shoptalk and crap—
　　Slack in work and slack in study,
　　It yells, "Free Speech," with its jaws all bloody.

Into the scene rushes Yu Xuanji, a Chinese poetess, 20, wearing pants, a blouse, a coat, and her hair in braids. She carries a flute. She halts before Mao's raised pistol.

MAO: Yu Xuanji, stop! Poet, salute
　　Our revolution with your flute!
　　See answers beyond question now:
　　The right music captures our foe!

　　[*Aside.*] Violence exudes a sly succulence—
　　Like violins serenading executions.

　　[*To Yu.*] Ink is too thin. Spill blood to write.

Trudeau intervenes, pushing aside Mao's arm.

TRUDEAU: [*To Mao.*] Why sour sweet parley with spite?

YU: Now, whose tongue sounds so lyrical?

TRUDEAU: [*Bowing.*] Pierre Trudeau—of Montreal.

MAO: A matador adventurer—
    A matinee, law professor!

TRUDEAU: [*To Mao.*] Speak sparkling quicksilver, don't wane to tin—
    Like some polymorphous politician!

MAO: Those who stymie political analysis
    Are condemned to suffer social paralysis.

YU: [*To Trudeau.*] You are livid lightning—
    And the vivid rainbow left by lightning.

TRUDEAU: You are the light lightning ignites.

MAO: Poets are privileged and pampered parasites.

YU: A poet's only useful as a poet.

MAO: Each one's an ink-and-paper bandit!

TRUDEAU: Chairman Mao, you're a poet: Where's your heart?
    Poetry is a helpful art.

YU: I will talk of freedom!

MAO: Does talk,
    Talk, talk, talk, talk, talk, talk, talk, talk,
    Feed those who swill watery muck?

    Monumental yapping retards
    Toppling statues on boulevards.

TRUDEAU: Don't snigger at poetry!

MAO: It depends.

YU: Poetry begins where lying ends.

MAO: Lays and ballets do best as bullets—
    Bullets for battles.

Trudeau plucks a flower and hands it to Yu.

TRUDEAU: Poetry is as useful as these petals.

Trudeau grabs the surprised Mao's gun. He pirouettes.

TRUDEAU: I will explain: In Palestine,
    Two bandits, to seize what was mine,
    Brandished daggers at my visage,
    But I astonished each savage
    By seizing one of their daggers,
    Then stabbed the air and staggered,
    Cried out poems, spewed mad madrigals,
    Alexandrines, octosyllables,
    So the bandits feared me insane—
    Or a saint—and so fled the terrain,
    Scramming into the desert sands,
    While I laughed loudly, yelled, and danced.

MAO: You've just plagiarized *Cyrano
    De Bergerac:* Act I, Scene vii.

YU: [*To Trudeau.*] I love its *éclat*, its *brio*!

TRUDEAU: [*To Yu.*] Your words elevate me to Heaven.

Mao wrests the gun away from Trudeau.

MAO: Firing squads accomplish more than bureaucrats:
    I trust devils more than I trust diplomats.

The State must mandate counterweights
And balance artists and elites.

A people's poet wields more than words:
Cannons, grenades, daggers, and swords!

[*Aside.*] What care I who lives or who dies,
So long as I—and China—rise!

Dropping her flower, Yu now seizes the gun from Mao.

YU: [*Aside.*] To make 'tiger' Mao meow and purr,
It takes a classic massacre …

A poet—by rote—of terror,
His style urges rape and murder.

His honesty is dishonest—
Merit meretricious—at its best.

TRUDEAU: [*Anxiously.*] Let's go forth now, chanting haikus
And albas and sonnets and epics and blues.

Mao embraces Yu—and regains his gun. Yu pushes Mao away.

MAO: Yu Xuanji, you'll have a soldier-poet's babies.

YU: I'd rather have scabies and rabies, scabies and rabies!

MAO: I like you: you are arrogant.

YU: Every poet is arrogant.

TRUDEAU: To incompetents, competent
People always seem arrogant.

Mao embraces Yu again.

MAO: Down with verse, that papery dove!
  Claim instead the freedom to love!

Yu shakes off Mao.

YU: Freedom to love is liberty
  A woman can rue bitterly.

MAO: I take Nanjing and set it free:
  And thus I remake history.

TRUDEAU: History's not for everyone—
  Chiang Kai-shek is surely done.

YU: Love history, and it loves back.

TRUDEAU: Just watch me, please. I don't look back.

*Mao, Trudeau, and Yu now waltz together in turn, with Mao's
pistol continuing to change hands. This dance is a tango.*

YU: You have to make history
  As gracefully as making love.

An explosion! Trudeau and Yu embrace. Mao regains his gun.

MAO: To war! I yearn for burning war!
  I cannot spurn hot, burning war!

Mao runs off. Trudeau continues to embrace Yu. She squirms free.

YU: I don't really know who you are—
  A French Canadian strayed far …

TRUDEAU: I study law—and love—and war.

Trudeau retrieves the flower and his backpack, then removes a jar.

TRUDEAU: Yu, my canteen yields caviar.

> Last Christmas Day, in India,
> While Pakistan split South Asia,
> I slurped caviar, gulped water,
> While musing on man-made slaughter.
> Let me spoon you this salt-sea fruit.

YU: I'll serenade you on my flute.

Yu sits beside Trudeau and plays her flute, releasing, unexpectedly, piano music into the air.

YU: Why bend Mao your bashful salute?
   He's no poet; he's just a brute.

Trudeau sniffs the flower, then kisses Yu.

YU: Ah, you're too cute for me to blame!

TRUDEAU: You're a beauty; a living flame!

DUET: If only we could make history
   Just by making love.
   Then maybe all human history
   Would chronicle love.

The scene ends with kissing and a welling up of anthemic, patriotic strings.

Scene ii: Fredericton, New Brunswick, April 1956

On the lawn of the University of New Brunswick, before a red brick monument emblazoned with the gold-letter slogan, "Poets' Corner," with apple blossoms impinging thereon, Trudeau, 36, sporting a cream-coloured suit, meets John Fitzgerald Kennedy, 38, a senator from Massachusetts. Kennedy wears a suit, a black tasselled cap, and gown. He carries a framed degree.

KENNEDY: Say, Pierre, I missed you at Hah-vahd!

TRUDEAU: [*Shrugging.*] That's why you won every award:
   My absence left you room to flower!

KENNEDY: [*Grinning.*] I continue to seize the hour!

Kennedy holds up the framed degree for inspection.

TRUDEAU: [*Reading.*] "John Fitzgerald Kennedy—
   Doctor of Laws": Honorary …

Trudeau shakes Kennedy's hand.

TRUDEAU: Senator Kennedy, congrats—
   Graduate, of Massachusetts,
   This April 1956
   At Fredericton, New Brunswick's
   University—New Brunswick.

KENNEDY: [*Shrugging.*] Thanks to Lord Beaverbrook's magic:
   He's spelled out this gilding parchment
   To burnish me for president,
   Crown me "royalty, American."

TRUDEAU: Election spurs adrenalin.

Kennedy leaps atop a rock, making it his pedestal. He removes his cap, gestures, and orates.

KENNEDY: To be smashing, chic, and naughty ...
    Styles politics, dashing, haughty!

Trudeau applauds Kennedy's energetic performance.

KENNEDY: Heed my speech, Pierre! Be king, not fool:
    Prestige blows smoke; power is a jewel.

    Live as Spartan as Superman,
    But jaunty, flaunting a bronze tan.

Trudeau now begins to spar, playfully, with Kennedy.

TRUDEAU: As a boy, my pulse jumped to greet
    Léo—"Kid"—Roy, champ of our street:
    No words explain triumph I felt,
    Grasping his Olympian belt.
    That golden trophy, blinding bright,
    Exuded searing, solar light.

    Inspired by Québec's boxing king—
    I danced into the punching ring:
    Papa shipped home four fists of gloves,
    Instructed me in Kid Roy's moves.

    [*Aside.*] I had to spar—to win Pa's love.

KENNEDY: [*Musing.*] Combat is love I can approve:
    Not truculence, but swashbuckling—
    Like a bass nixing a duckling.

    Act with *chutzpah*—like Hemingway,
    Shooting white foam or wingèd clay.

My ballet is battle—the grace
Of malice, coup, and *coup de grâce* ...

Life's a boxing match—or a bullfight,
Where right succeeds through leonine might.

TRUDEAU: True: all rich kids come up callow,
But heroes hulk, big-hearted, brave.

What mountain can quicksand swallow?
What aristocrat lives a slave?

Trudeau dances about.

TRUDEAU: I'll laugh at fame, ignore the bank,
Annoy all fools, and cowards spank.

Come misfortune, I'll gladly shrug:
The pugnacious man's always smug.

I'll spout forth sonnets with my fists—
And let my feet add emphasis.

Exuberance must never pall:
I'll rise highest—or not at all![12]

KENNEDY: Politics mirrors acts of war:
One out-muscles each contender.

[*Winking.*] And virgins, unspeakably sweet,
Toss moist panties at your feet.

Pierre, man, grant politics a whirl:
Rack up votes! Sack girl upon girl!

---

12   Cf. Rostand, *Cyrano de Bergerac*, II.viii.368.

TRUDEAU: You score a point: I would be thrilled.

Kennedy checks his watch.

KENNEDY: [*Shivering.*] Fredericton's cold, April-chilled.
   I'll jet to Havana to rest.

Kennedy shakes hands with Trudeau. He dons his cap, and moves toward the thrashing sound of a helicopter preparing for takeoff.

TRUDEAU: [*Waving.*] Don't forget to free the oppressed!

KENNEDY: [*Waving and shouting.*]
   Oppression ends by changing law.

TRUDEAU: "*Les révolutions justes sont le châtiment
   des mauvais rois.*"[13]

Lights down.

---

13 This inscription appears on a Bayonne, France, monument to the martyrs of 1831.

ACT II

News has a kind of mystery.
GOODMAN

Scene i: Havana, Cuba, April 1960

A rainbow fiesta of tropical pastels warms the set. Trudeau, now 40, appears in Bermuda shorts, dark sunglasses, sandals, and a mandarin-collar shirt. He sips rum and smokes Freudian cigars with Fidel Castro, 34, bearded and dressed in Cuban army fatigues, with a pistol at his side. His aide is Lt. Neruda, Afro-Cuban, 34, who also packs a gun. Trudeau's canoe sits in the background.

CASTRO: Señor Trudeau, "Ahoy," sings Havana!
  Magically, you've canoed from Florida—
  Like a *guerrillero*. How brave—
  You, solo, shooting shark-jawed waves!

  [*Aside.*] Here's a man built of blood, not martinis:
  His study's dusty; he wafts up woods and seas.

  Lieutenant Neruda, a round of rum!

NERUDA: Trudeau, knock back only our blackest rum ...

Neruda pours. Trudeau, Castro, and Neruda click glasses.

CASTRO: Love this lacquered, lustrous blackness!

NERUDA: This blackly black, blackest blackness!

TRUDEAU: *¡Viva Cuba y el pueblo cubano!*

CASTRO: *¡Viva la amistad cubana-canadiense!*

Everyone drinks.

TRUDEAU: This April 1960,
    Señor Castro, I had to see
    Your revolution: It excites!
    Québec's is just too quiet—like kites.

NERUDA: Yet, Québec's revolt rears a score—
    The *joual* of *"les nègres du nord."*

CASTRO: [*To Trudeau.*] Maybe you're just some playboy militant,
    A dilly-dallying, shilly-shallying dilettante?

NERUDA: Or a groupie to Cuba's jubilant liberation?
    Or a tourist ogling "Caribbean tribulation"?

TRUDEAU: For myself, I just had to see
    Why Cuba so riles the Yankee.

CASTRO: We drive America crazy, drive Yanks crazy,
    Because we drove the Mafia back to Miami.

NERUDA: We cashiered casinos and gave
    Poor Cubans cash!

TRUDEAU: That was rash!

NERUDA: Brave!

CASTRO: [*To Trudeau.*] Do you like the rum? This cigar?

TRUDEAU: It's exquisite, famous, five-star.

CASTRO: I like your prime minister who scares
    Television and U.S. ears.

TRUDEAU: You mean Diefenbaker! He's fine—
   He backs a bill of rights I'd sign.

CASTRO: He looks a sorry sight, and speaks
   Such big words his big head shakes.

NERUDA: Señor Trudeau, you aren't—*sí*—a Marxist?

TRUDEAU: I like Groucho Marx ...

NERUDA: Be serious!

TRUDEAU: [*Aside.*] My father died! He died! I feel outside everything!
   [*To Neruda.*] I know what it means to feel outside everything.

NERUDA: Naw, *buckra*,[14] white boy, you ain't black:
   You're just another gringo outta Québec.
   Decide now whose side you're on!

TRUDEAU: I'm on the outside—
   Unless I've got a girl at my side!

CASTRO: Pierre, you're one brash, "bourgie" hombre.

TRUDEAU: Fidel, I'll down one more *Cuba libre*.

Trudeau holds up his glass; Castro pours.

CASTRO: In Harlem, I met Malcolm X,
   That Black Islamic intellect:
   We agreed we poor need atom bombs all our own,
   So profiteers and parasites get overthrown.

TRUDEAU: The Canadian genius
   Is no army defines us.

---

14 Try also *buckaroo* (Af-Am.) or *toubab* (Fr. Ant.).

CASTRO: [*Guffawing.*] The U.S. Army affronts Canada—
    Just as it confronts Korea!

NERUDA: If Kennedy troops, here he dies,
    Under our boots and machetes.

Neruda picks up a machete and waves it.

    His unwholesome face, like an ass,
    Opens to let some slick feces pass—
    Some intimate obscenity,
    Debaucherous debility …

CASTRO: *Gracias*, Lieutenant Neruda—
    Bid our boss cook broil barracuda.

Neruda departs. Trudeau and Castro light cigars.

TRUDEAU: It's good to swill your rum
    And smoke your cigars.

CASTRO: We'll skin-dive, flush with rum,
    Under light-plush stars.

TRUDEAU: Surely you must conduct the State.

CASTRO: We'll clean machine guns Soviet.

Castro picks up two machine guns and hands one to Trudeau, who hefts and aims it. Castro smiles approvingly.

CASTRO: Let peaceniks puff of beatnik love—
    I trust in my Kalashnikov!

Neruda runs back in. He salutes Castro.

NERUDA: Yanks attacking the Bay of Pigs!
  We're whacking them: they dance death jigs!

  They sweat piss, then blood urinate:
  Our guns gnaw them from foot to pate!

CASTRO: If they want war, the day will dawn
  When we will hang each Yankee son,
  And all imperialists face purge,
  Making New York New Nuremburg.

TRUDEAU: Once disaster starts, there's no end:
  Corpses pile up; maggots unbend;
  The stink and rot appall; all screech—
  "Set fire to our dead"; smoke shrouds speech ...

CASTRO: Serve Kennedy an Austerlitz
  In the swamps of the Bay of Pigs!

NERUDA: Repair that gross monstrosity,
  Fix insolent pomposity!

CASTRO: All power flows from the barrel of a gun!

NERUDA: All power flows from the barrel of a gun!

*Castro shakes hands with Trudeau, grabs a machine gun, and dons
a helmet, then runs offstage with Neruda. Sound of gunfire in the
distance.*

TRUDEAU: Who is shooting whom? Why? What for?
  In history's fog and ice-cold war?

*Trudeau stretches out on the lounge chair, and continues to smoke
and drink.*

Scene ii: Montréal, Québec, July 1960

Biddles nightclub in Montréal. Blue light tints lounge tables.
Roscoe Robertson, 30-ish, a black jazz musician, in tux and bowtie,
plinks a piano. Simone Cixous, 25, in black ensemble and beret,
approaches. She sports a camera, a notebook, and a pen.

CIXOUS: Roscoe Robertson, where's Trudeau?
    Have you any clue? Do you know?

ROBERTSON: Simone, Pierre's a Montrealer—as
    Unpredictable as free jazz.

    From *Native Son* to *Invisible Man*,
    He shifts like ectoplasm—or Peter Pan.

    His life *is* his art; a canvas
    Shimmering black-and-white contrasts.

CIXOUS: I hear he schmoozed with Mao in Red China,
    Then drilled our wildcat, Asbestos miners
    In proverbs from Marx-Lenin-Mao:
    The strikers cheered and chewed their chow.

    [*Swooning.*] I'm chatting him up for *Châtelaine*,
    I want the August 60 cover.
    He seems so sexy—for a brain.

    [*Aside.*] I lust to become his lover:
    A bestseller in hardcover,
    He must prove an epic lover.

Cixous leans against the piano, then 'wines' ('Trini'-style) as
Robertson plays.

ROBERTSON: Pierre's a macho aristocrat,
    A dialectic acrobat,

No politician—a Ph.D.,
A jet-setting, Rat Pack dandy,
A cold-as-dry-ice rationalist,
A photogenic Platonist,
A boxer who quotes poetry—
Chic as Cassius Clay "Ali"—
A go-go, day-glo cavalier,
A ritzy, glitzy, Warhol superstar,
A Sphinx-like Statue of Liberty—
Napoleon as Castiglione—
And he's got the gall of Charles de Gaulle:
He's J.F.K. of Montreal.

A *Playboy* swinger,
A 3-D thinker,
A white Negro clone:
He's a rolling stone!

CIXOUS: Oh, his photos look so damned dramatic!
　　　He's *un charmeur*, charming, charismatic …

Adonis—or Don Quixote?
Don Juan—or Wile E. Coyote?

An enigma, a prodigy?
A most eccentric oddity?

*Trudeau, in dark sunglasses and a white linen suit, enters and
approaches Robertson. He eyes the still-dancing Cixous.*

ROBERSTON: *Bonjour*, Pierre, *comment ça va?*

TRUDEAU: *Bien*, Roscoe.

ROBERTSON: 　　　　　　　*Tu es toujours comme ça.*
　　　This lady seeks a word with you.

Robertson plays the piano, while Cixous and Trudeau chat and cha-cha-cha.

CIXOUS: Um, *je m'appelle Simone Cixous.*

TRUDEAU: *Enchanté! Vous êtes très jolie.*
  So you'd like to interview me?
  But you reporters are hard to trust.

CIXOUS: But you're also a journalist.

TRUDEAU: "I only trust the press I own":
  I quote Lasalle ... Or Emerson?

CIXOUS: What do you study, Pierre Trudeau?

TRUDEAU: Karate, jiu-jitsu, judo:
  I like to throw you journalists!

CIXOUS: I see you read French surrealists!
  But do you read Alice Munro?

TRUDEAU: I prefer Marilyn Monroe.

CIXOUS: What do you think of Parliament?

TRUDEAU: A good, strong, English cigarette.

CIXOUS: What's your political analysis?

TRUDEAU: It's an ass—to be horsewhipped by sadists.

CIXOUS: You stage *l'homme politique* as Rasputin!

TRUDEAU: I prefer to spend treasured oxygen
  Skiing, swimming, not on claptrap—
  Unparliamentary, parliamentary crap.

CIXOUS: Is each politico a joke?

TRUDEAU: In a coma, they run amok!

Parliament's the Playboy Mansion:
Each feather bed there's a pension.

The Tories are piglets, screeching, screeching.
The Grits are bloodsuckers, leeching, leeching.

CIXOUS: But you could have gilded success—
Sir Gazillionaire—glamorous.

TRUDEAU: Parliament's a bundle of posteriors
Bugling profundities or tooting errors.

CIXOUS: Lord, don't stonewall me like a cop!
Can I interview you in person?

TRUDEAU: Where does melodic applause stop
And brash, cackling catcalls begin?

Trudeau bows, kisses Cixous, waves to Robertson, and vanishes.

CIXOUS: That man exudes so much panache,
He makes me shiver, ache, and blush.
I wonder where he's off to now?

ROBERTSON: Back to Red China, to powwow with Mao.

Cocktail piano percolates.

Scene iii: Beijing, China, 1 October 1960

In a study, Mao, now 67, in military uniform, meets Trudeau,
sporting a scarf, beret, and sports jacket. Between them is a globe
on a table. They sit in gigantic armchairs. Muffled cheers underline
this holiday honouring the founding of the People's Republic of
China. A chorus unfolds popular song.

CHORUS: [*Offstage.*] History's fuelled by food and blood.
    Mao's Communists cook up soul food.
    Mao's ginseng poems revive our blood:
    Mao's philosophy spoons us food.

    We winnow bread and wine from words:
    Our religion now is eating.
    We don't waste lilies in verses:
    We devour them at our feasting.

MAO: The globe crawls with rapists, pirates,
    But fate's fatal to fatalists.
    Power is the only fact that matters!
    (I clout a jerk, his braincase splatters.)
    I say, *"Après moi, le déluge."*
    I've read *Innocents en Chine rouge*—
    Your *Innocents in Red China*—
    Celebrating liberated China.

TRUDEAU: And I've read *Essays on Philosophy,*
    Tussling with your poignant theory
    That freedom struggle is ceaseless.
    Our struggle is non-stop, endless.

MAO: In capitalist plutocracy,
    No hegemony without money.

TRUDEAU: [*Aside.*] I hear Papa when I hear Mao speak
    Truths more antique than Chinese or Greek.

Muffled cheers intrude from without.

TRUDEAU: In Québec, maggots of lawyers
    Bask in cesspools of corruption.

    A pus-paste, bag of dung and phlegm:
    Our premier. Mud's his emblem.

    Vomit geysers, shitty blowholes,
    Venomous vents, foul fumaroles,
    Dirty our white legislature
    With diarrhea: discourse impure …

MAO: I like a leader who's clear about what he hates!
    His bloodbaths scour and polish his state.

TRUDEAU: Québec sways between *brasserie et cathédrale.*

MAO: Workers think pain is natural.

TRUDEAU: Th'Assembly scripts fits and blood clots,
    Pratfalls, catcalls, curtain calls, plots.

MAO: The dialectic declares, "Decapitate
    Reprobate foes of the People's state."

TRUDEAU: So infamously difficult,
    To be oneself—*and* head a cult …

MAO: Toadies' mouths suck like a slut's crotch:
    Nurse them on drops of poisoned Scotch.

TRUDEAU: Our atmosphere perspires pure fire:
    Pyromaniacs spark each pyre.

MAO: These rabid vermin sting and bite—
    Hostile as hosted parasite—

To lessen majesty to jest,
Stab their betters through back and chest.

From gibbets, hang bigots in hosts.
If no gibbets, we'll use lampposts.

TRUDEAU: False atoms of authority
Fraction, split, before your army.

MAO: Torture is art and craft of state
(Evil liberals tolerate).
To imp our foes to tears and howls,
Disembowl em! Castrate cabals!
To buttress mass democracy
—dissidents as enemy.
Crucify em! Don't sit pretty!
Batter em til your hands drip bloody!
(Rip up butterflies—they've no worth:
Let their torn wings colour the earth!)
Surgical cutting liberates
Governors from sick'ning debates.
My duty is to make truth hurt—
To vipers thrust down under dirt.

Trudeau pours more wine for himself and Mao.

TRUDEAU: What do girls dream of in China?

MAO: Our victory in Indochina!
This world mounts a crisis circus.

Muffled cheers intrude from without. The wine is drunk.

TRUDEAU: More wine and more analysis!

Trudeau holds up his glass and Mao pours.

MAO: Every Canadian should swoon
   At the name of Norman Bethune
   And submit his life to people.

TRUDEAU: I can be no man's disciple.

MAO: No isolate individual
   Exercises power palpable.

TRUDEAU: What if I rise by people's votes?

MAO: Trudeau, melt down gold for bullets:
   They beautify more than ballots!
   Democracy's a game for dolts.

TRUDEAU: I am, perhaps, a naïve guy—
   To trust silly, slimy, smelly,
   Noisy, nasty democracy!

MAO: What you trust is plutocracy.

   Emperors must be unhorsed,
   And stable boys enthroned—by force.

TRUDEAU: Are stable boys fit to govern?

MAO: Our proletariat is sovereign.

Muffled cheers intrude from without.

TRUDEAU: I go now to get drunk on lotus,
         Then tarantella
   With peasant virgins gone hoarse,
         Moaning the deaths of dahlias.

*Mao rises, as does Trudeau, bowing, and both exit the study.
Cheers well up.*

Scene iv: Beijing, China, 1 October 1960

Party lights compose a Mardi Gras scene, scarlet with Chinese lanterns and flags. Trudeau cavorts with a moon-masked, young woman—really Yu—here in a green polka-dot dress. Her two braids fly. She carries a flute.

TRUDEAU: Ah, Maiden Moon, I feel I know you now.
   Come, let's cuddle.

YU: [*Giggling.*]   Don't you kowtow to Mao?

TRUDEAU: Your voice! I've cherished it before—

YU: At Nanjing, in the civil war.

TRUDEAU: Eleven years ago—gone swiftly!

YU: Tonight's October 1st, 1960.

Yu removes her mask and plays her flute. Trudeau performs a somersault.

TRUDEAU: Oh, girl, in the polka-dot dress,
   You are Yu, enchanting poetess.

YU: [*Aside.*] All dream of undreamt-of coitus.

TRUDEAU: I wish I were the Sun King now.
   Might I command your moon somehow?

YU: The sun cannot hold long the moon.

   My light—too bright—will make you swoon,
   While I hover, remote, above.

TRUDEAU: Claim—like Mao—the freedom to love!

Trudeau and Yu turn, kissing as they do so.

TRUDEAU: Encore.

YU: *Zai lai.*[15]

TRUDEAU: Again.

YU: Again.

TRUDEAU: Encore.

YU: *Zai lai.*

The scene closes with a continuous kiss.

---

15 This Mandarin Chinese word means "again." Dr. Ming Xie of the Department of English, University of Toronto, states, "The Chinese vowel *ai* is narrower than *I* in English, somewhere between *bad* and *bide*. The stress falls on *zai*" (letter, 2 May VI).

ACT III

Freedom! Justice! Equality!
THULANI DAVIS, X

Scene i: Mooréa, Tahiti, 12 February 1968

In a flower-print, Tahitian shirt, dark sunglasses (angled on his head), and trunks, Trudeau, 48, lounges on a chaise longue, reading Plato's Republic. Margaret, 20, in a flower-power bikini and a wrap as sheer and as frothing as champagne, approaches him. She wears a garland of Tahitian flowers.

MARGARET: Aren't you the Justice Minister?

TRUDEAU: Not so loud! I'm undercover.

MARGARET: That's why you're here in Tahiti?

TRUDEAU: No one here should recognize me.

MARGARET: I eyed you on television when you said
   Government has no business in my bed.
   You lassoed my vote—just for that.
   [*Aside.*] At love, you unleash a wildcat?

Margaret snaps the elastic waistline of Trudeau's swim trunks.

TRUDEAU: Hey! Careful! I'd like children yet.

MARGARET: [*Laughing.*] Relax! Don't act a square! I've met
   Every living cabinet minister!

TRUDEAU: Otherwise would be sinister!

MARGARET: [*Laughing.*] I didn't mean it as it sounds!
　　You're a screwy, soft egghead!

TRUDEAU: 　　　　　　　　　Zounds!
　　You're Lolita—gone Tahitian.

MARGARET: No, I'm a British Columbian:
　　Margaret, daughter of Sincere,
　　The ex-fisheries minister.
　　I've been watching you dive. You're good!
　　Whatcha doin with this old book?

*Margaret pushes Trudeau, who drops the book. She runs. He
chases and catches her, then holds her in his arms.*

TRUDEAU: Like some Vandal or some beatnik,
　　You've just trashed Plato's Republic!

MARGARET: Here, in green, perfumed Tahiti,
　　His gospel's a musty ditty.

TRUDEAU: May I illuminate his plot, explain?

Trudeau tries to kiss Margaret, but she squirms away, teasingly.

MARGARET: Plato ain't simpatico (unlike champagne):
　　His pizzazz fizzles out—like tap water!

TRUDEAU: But you sizzle with dynamite hauteur—
　　That diamond patina of martinis.

MARGARET: You old boys lust to untie bikinis!

TRUDEAU: Your bikini mirrors that atoll
　　Split in half by Yankee H-bombs.

Lights down: Spotlight on each as they move apart and speak separately.

MARGARET: [*Aside.*] My charts, soulful and astrological,
   Foresaw I'd meet a man mercurial,
   Venusian, earthy, saturnine, and martial:
   A carnal canticle.

TRUDEAU: [*Aside.*] Here she is—so, so beautiful,
   So challenging, so pulsating!
   Rosé rapture excites turmoil—
   Extra joy! My heart's gyrating!

Spotlight off as Margaret and Trudeau return to face-to-face conversation.

MARGARET: Hmm, I suspect you sport a *roué* aura …
   [*Aside.*] *Bwana* wanna make fauna in my flora!

TRUDEAU: A drum and rum heat up music.
   You incarnate *mana*—Polynesian magic.

MARGARET: You're not so old when you're excited!

TRUDEAU: What?

MARGARET: [*Laughing.*] Do I feel something rigid?

TRUDEAU: [*Aside.*] Now spring springs open every gate,
   This February 68:
   I feel the future is being born!
   I'm embracing April in my autumn.

MARGARET: [*Aside.*] His stallion style kicks down each stall:
   Can my coy rose enmesh, enthrall—
   Venusian, earthy, saturnine, and martial,
   This man canonical?

Trudeau kisses Margaret's brow lightly.

TRUDEAU: I hold a nymph, a sylph in silk,
　　Rich chestnut-tressed, snow-fresh—like milk.
　　So pliable, mobile, and nubile—
　　Plato recast as the *Kama Sutra*.

MARGARET: You're alabaster-coated iron—
　　To wax metaphorical.

Trudeau and Margaret kiss.

TRUDEAU: You are so sinuously,
　　Virtuoso beautiful—
　　A woman as much an earthquake
　　As Josephine Baker when she shakes.

MARGARET: It takes moxie
　　To be sexy.

TRUDEAU: [*Aside.*] God of poets, mix curses, sighs,
　　If tears should e'er obscure her eyes.

Margaret takes Trudeau's hand in hers. They kiss again.

DUET: We'll touch, retouch, until, *touché*,
　　We marry *poutine* and sushi.

　　Everything we do, we'll make news—
　　Our love will make history muse.

The lovers kiss.

Scene ii: Paris, France, 21 March 1968

Suited in eye-scalding scarlet (from beret to shoe), Robertson sits with Trudeau, who sports a turban and Nehru jacket. A café.

ROBERTSON: Let's lunch right here—amid these flowers.

TRUDEAU: You mean the girls—primping like flowers.

ROBERTSON: It's Paris in the spring, Pierre!

TRUDEAU: This March 68 steams like summer.

ROBERTSON: Fess up about this chick you've met.

TRUDEAU: Only wine—
    Constantly nothing but wine—
    Blush wine for this champagne brunette:
    I pamper her with *rosé* wine.

    Sunned in honey, her svelte shape satisfies.

ROBERTSON: [*Laughing.*]
    Man, look at you! Your eyes are as damp as Venice!

    You'll play Batman & Catwoman,
    Jack & Jackie, Baudelaire & Jeanne!

TRUDEAU: Roscoe, are you some damned Romantic?
    Stick to your piano!

ROBERTSON: [*Laughing.*] Talk politics!
    You really wanna be prime minister?

TRUDEAU: Our responsibility to the past
    Is to be contemporary.

ROBERTSON: Canada's so horse-and-buggy ...
　　　　But it'll risk a "sports-car" leader,
　Cause we all crave Kennedy,
　　　　　A turbo-charged, fuel-injected speedster.

TRUDEAU: [*Shrugging.*] I count the hydra-headed crowd
　No more important than a cloud.

ROBERTSON: The cranks will slam you as a Communist!

TRUDEAU: The true Marxists are Santa Claus and Christ.

　Besides, the duty of government is to be fair and just.

ROBERTSON: No, the *beauty* of government is to uplift and heal.

　But I think you'll make a fun P.M.:
　TV cameras will eye you, a.m. to p.m.—

　　　　You're our linguistic
　Mulatto; a bilingual,
　　　　　Half-n-half Canuck.

　Mr. In-Between—
　　　　　A duet of splintered mirrors,
　Mixed identities ...

TRUDEAU: Apply Norm Mailer:
　　　　　Am I "white Negro"—a French-Scotch
　Soul on clear, black ice?

ROBERTSON: Austin Clarke insists
　　　　　You've got West Indian *chutzpah*—
　And style like a king.

Robertson reaches inside his jacket and withdraws two huge spliffs. Trudeau takes one and sniffs it lovingly.

TRUDEAU: Canada's *canards*
　　　Must quit foxholes and anthills,
And soar to the stars!

ROBERTSON: These sublime "cigars"—
　　　Jamaican scrolls—lift up thought,
Summon down sunlight.

Robertson and Trudeau both smoke up.

TRUDEAU: We're Rastafari—
　　　Takin weed like it's church wine—
Some *truly* "holy" smoke.

ROBERTSON: In the spirit of
　　　Jimmy Cliff and *bad* James Brown,
Inhale and inhale!

The two men puff away and polish off the wine.

Scene iii: Ottawa, Ontario, 6 April 1968

Spotlight on a giant, prophetic photograph, from April 1967, of Trudeau, John Turner, and Jean Chrétien, all new cabinet ministers of Prime Minister Pearson (also visible), each of whom will later become prime minister in his own right. The portrait vanishes to the sound of cheers, horns, kazoos, and other hoopla. Before an empty podium festooned with microphones stand Margaret and Cixous (both in miniskirts), and Robertson, carrying a Trudeau sign. A backdrop appears: an all-encompassing mirror.

CIXOUS: Margaret, rumours circle you
　Are Trudeau's lover. Are they true?

MARGARET: Miss Cixous, you're a reporter.

CIXOUS: Trudeau's become prime minister,
  So his private life's public now.

ROBERTSON: Can it! He's here! Trudeau! Trudeau!

ALL: Trudeau! Trudeau! Trudeau! Trudeau!

MARGARET: Pierre! Pierre! Pierre! Pierre! Pierre! Pierre! Pierre!
  Pierre!

ROBERTSON: He's here! He's here!

CIXOUS: He's here! He's here!

*Amid confetti and detonating flashbulbs, Trudeau, in a black,
three-piece suit, with a carnation on one lapel, dashes to the
podium. He smiles and waves at his supporters, a trio of Cixous,
Margaret, and Robertson.*

TRIO: Trudeau, Trudeau!
  It's spring! It's spring!
  Trudeau, Trudeau—
  Vote him king!

  Trudeau, Trudeau!
  Trudeaumania!
  Trudeau, Trudeau!
  O Canada!

TRUDEAU: Open all the windows! The sun
  Wants in! It's April once again.
  How beautiful is Ottawa
  In the spring—for all Liberals!

ROBERTSON: [*Aside.*] Every Tory
  Is history!

Every Tory:
History!

CIXOUS: [*Aside.*] His manner's "blond"—
    Shiny, a gem—
    Voters respond,
    "We don't deserve him."

TRUDEAU: Though April sunlight streams and gleams,
    Though exquisite are all our dreams,
    Canada's not perfect, we all know—
    These four thousand miles mapped by snow.
    But iced geography allows
    Only a fierce people to flower.

MARGARET: [*Aside.*] He's a man's man,
    A man's man,
    A lady's man,
    Lady's man,

    And a poet's poet,
    Poet of poets,
    Dictator of
    Love sonnets.

TRUDEAU: No school could teach me patriot
    Love, but I feel in my bones the riot
    Of snow over tundra, field, and moor,
    This land's ocean-vast, sky-high rapture.

ROBERTSON: [*Aside.*] Irving Layton
    Says Pierre's the first
    Canuck chief worth
    Sassinatin.

CIXOUS: [*Aside.*] He's supernova,
    The bright "New Wave"—

Bossa nova,
Nouvelle vague.

TRUDEAU: Our Canada glows *rouge* and white
(Maple leaves red on snow delight)—
But Earth shudders and shakes with hate
This April 1968:
Two days past, Martin Luther King
Was shot through the throat, just for dreaming
Of a truly Just Society—
Exactly what Canada must be.
The U.S. war in Vietnam
Baptizes infants in napalm.
And, here at home, Québec protests
That "Anglos" are "imperialists."

MARGARET: [*Aside.*] Pierre's the cream
Of Liberals!
Our starry dream,
Liberals!

TRUDEAU: We'll deploy counterweights (like Mao),
Balance Québec and Ottawa.
Canada must not become at all
A Confederation—mean, provincial.

ROBERTSON: [*Aside.*] The people thrill
At his guile,
Kennedy skill,
James Bond style.

TRUDEAU: The Age of Aquarius decrees
Our Golden Age, *pace* Rome and Greece.

Let us rear rose gardens along avenues—
Tender reveries that render revenues.

MARGARET: [*Aside.*] All women trill
  At his smile,
  His looks that thrill,
  His cool style.

TRUDEAU: The Constitution's a jar of worms—
  Each word wriggles, each clause squirms.

CIXOUS: [*Aside.*] No number-crunching,
  Doughnut-munching,
  Hotdog eater:
  He's live theatre.

TRUDEAU: Let us adventure together.
  Canada's *nada* without adventure!

CHORUS: Right speech! Right reach! Right plans! Right stands!
  Right schemes! Right dreams! Right songs! Right wrongs!

TRUDEAU: Come, dally with me,
  Ally with me,
  Rally to me!
  O, rally!

CIXOUS: [*Aside.*] His go-go girls all go gaga:
  They cue a frou-frou brouhaha!

*With a flower and stem between his teeth, Trudeau pirouettes
offstage. Cheers.*

Scene iv: Gatineau, Québec, 16 April 1968

*In battle fatigues and sandals, Trudeau stands alone on a forest
beach, his backpack and canoe nearby. With a hatchet, he chops up
wood for a campfire.*

TRUDEAU: This April 1968,
    These charted stars narrate my fate:
    I become prime minister now
    To headline a carnival show
    And prostitute my privacy
    To face and eye publicity—
    Mother's milk of all politics
    (Alcohol for alcoholics)—
    And roll out finest folderol—
    Speeches as solid as a hole—
    Branding Pierre a Pierrot—
    Un idiot on radio,
    A metaphysical misfit,
    A blank-faced, black-comic wit …

    Elastic, plastic "alabast,"
    My image will be telecast
    In vapid metamorphoses—
    Evaporating by degrees—
    Or played as eunuch or as whore,
    Betrayed by sketchy metaphor,
    Til I'm scorned, condemned, tarred as liar—
    A "hypocrite in Anglo hire."

    (Québec shadows each Québécois:
    It's my blood, my pride, *not* my law.)

    But what leader can I become—
    A "coupé-and-canoe P.M."?
    How can I foster liberty?
    (I've freed, so far, just P.E.T.!)
    I've no mortgage, no family,
    Not one responsibility,
    I've floated free of destiny—
    A playboy, now pushing fifty!

Trudeau builds and lights a fire.

Though late to blossom, I am new—
Symbolizing futures come due.
(History dwells in a brothel,
But the future stays virginal.)

I, my government, have no past—
Our practice must greyed myth recast.
Whatever I try will birth news,
Foes antagonize, friends confuse.

Trudeau kneels and prays—in the Buddhist fashion.

Papa, I pray you see your son
Procure secular election—
No, not among the blessèd saints,
But still elect, punching *sans* feints,
Against super-sized rats and snakes,
Flatterers so loud the air shakes,
And wild, anarchic, rowdy chaps
Who clap for government collapse.

But in myself, I've all I need—
To master Parliament—and lead.
Mon esprit de contradiction
Spells my balanced constitution.

I'll forge a rule dreamt by Shakespeare,
Not risk the fate of damned Robespierre.

Trudeau stands and looks skyward.

I spy the stars of destiny:
They are warm—and, oh, so shiny!

Lights down.

Scene v: Montréal, Québec, 24 June 1968

In Place Ville-Marie, girded by skyscrapers, stands a lone microphone. Cixous (in a new miniskirt) and Robertson mill about, awaiting Trudeau's arrival. Lighting echoes 60s psychedelia.

ROBERTSON: Trudeau's sole election promise
  Is to warm to China's communists.

CIXOUS: His campaign slogan, "It's Spring!"
  Means just about anything.

ROBERTSON: It signifies success in 68:
  It makes you exult, exhilarate.

CIXOUS: He'll snatch June 25th's election.
  Count pollsters 100% certain.

The whop-whop of a helicopter landing cuts off conversation.

ROBERTSON: This Montreal crowd spans so big
  Trudeau whirls in by whirligig.

Amid cheers and boos, Trudeau, sport-jacketed, rose-corsaged, runs to the microphone. Margaret attempts to kiss him, but he nudges her away. Flowers arc through the air. But Jacques Fanon, 30, in sandals and a plaid shirt, lobs a beer bottle at Trudeau. It lands harmlessly at his feet. Fanon shakes his fist.

FANON: *Trudeau au poteau!*[16] Pierre to the gallows!
  Trudeau au poteau! Hang him high!
  Trudeau au poteau! Pierre to the gallows!
  Trudeau au poteau! Traitors die!

---

16 A *poteau* is, in English, a post, especially one used to hold a condemned man upright before a firing squad. However, its gallows connotation suits Montréal's riotous night of 24 June 1968.

ROBERTSON: Damn your bitch mouth! Let Trudeau speak!

FANON: What he talks is shit: Is shit *chic?*

CIXOUS: Police will plague your policy.

ROBERTSON: But not today! Pierre *est ici.*

FANON: *Trudeau au poteau!* Hang him high!
   Trudeau au poteau! Traitors die!

TRUDEAU: I ask that drunken, loutish clown
   Who craves to bully, shout me down,
   Have you read Mao or Montesquieu?
   If not, then who, the fuck, are you?

CIXOUS: Pierre, did you curse? Did you swear?

TRUDEAU: It's possible you didn't hear:
   I said, "Fuddle duddle," that's all.

FANON: Trudeau said, "Fuck off!" Shit! What gall!

TRUDEAU: Fuddle duddle! Fuddle duddle!
   All I said was "Fuddle duddle."

ROBERTSON: [*To Fanon.*] If Pierre didn't say, "Fuck off," I will:
   Fuck off, asshole!

FANON: You bloody stool!

TRUDEAU: [*Aside.*] That lousy swine couldn't've heard
   Me say, "Eat shit": "*Mange de la merde!*"

Sound of scattered applause, cheers, boos.

TRUDEAU: Friends, Canadians, patriots,
 Quebeckers, friends, compatriots,
 Given the thousands of you here,
 My policies must be popular.

CIXOUS: [*Aside.*] It looks like he's stepped from a T.V.
 And into a Beatles concert.

ROBERTSON: [*Aside.*] Liberty! Peace! Equality!

MARGARET: [*Aside.*] Revolution's the orgasm of history!

ROBERTSON: P! E! T!

FANON: L! S! D![17]

ROBERTSON: P! E! T!

FANON: [*Aside.*] P-E-T spells out *pet,* his stench—
 This smart-ass breaks wind he calls "French."

TRUDEAU: To separatists, all you snivellers,
 Brainless dogs, and toothless tigers,
 I hear your bass tongues spit and hiss
 Like cobras, bray like jackasses.

CIXOUS: [*Aside.*] His tirade pleasures tyranny.

ROBERTSON: [*Aside.*] Participatory Democracy!

TRUDEAU: Vietnam had its Têt[18] turbulence,
 France had its May disturbance,
 Czechoslovakia's Prague Spring is
 Encircled by the Soviets,

---

17 LSD or Lysergic diethylamide acid.
18 On 30–31 January 1968, the North Vietnamese Army launched a massive guerilla
 assault, within South Vietnam, during the Vietnamese New Year, or Têt.

But in Canada we enjoy
Prospects of a Just Society.

CIXOUS: [*Aside.*] What is his "Just Society"?

ROBERTSON: [*Aside.*] Liberty! Peace! Equality!

MARGARET: [*Aside.*] A plastic flower is society!

FANON: *Trudeau au poteau!* Hang him high!
Trudeau au poteau! Traitors die!

TRUDEAU: [*Shaking his fist.*] To that miscreant, I must say
He despises democracy!

[*Aside.*] Policing him will be my policy.

Lights down on everyone. Spotlight on Trudeau, who leaves the stage and approaches Fanon, who is also in the spotlight.

TRUDEAU: Who the hell do you think you are, pal?

FANON: [*Shouting.*] *Je suis Jacques Fanon de Montréal!*

TRUDEAU: Emotionalism emaciates …
It thins out thought.

FANON: Nationalism's natural—
It's our birthright.

TRUDEAU: And so you're boisterous as a bomb:
Cause your thoughts don't add up, they don't count.

FANON: I say you're a Judas to Québec, *un "Oncle Tom,"*
A two-faced, white Rhodesian of Westmount.

TRUDEAU: You hurl dagger-sharp words at me,
   but they boomerang and smite your face.
Your blizzard invective melts in a day,
   but my sunlit laws gleam on and on.
Do you crave glory? Do you wish to be quoted?
   I will give you trouble! I will snarl truths!

FANON: You bull for Big Business and pig-bosses:
 You shill for the mob, you gull the masses!

 Your all-purpose, pinstriped persona
 Camouflages a foul piranha.

TRUDEAU: What if I sic the army on your class?

FANON: What if I dyn'mite your mailbox?
 What if I pelt your face with rocks?

TRUDEAU: What if I thrust bayonets up your ass?

FANON: *O, non, non, non!*

TRUDEAU: Oh, yes, yes, yes!

Trudeau flips Fanon the 'finger' and returns to his podium. Fanon returns the rude gesture. Lights up on everyone.

FANON: *Trudeau au poteau!* Pierre to the gallows!
 Trudeau au poteau! Pierre to the gallows!

ROBERTSON: [*Aside.*] Liberty! Peace! Equality!

CIXOUS: [*Aside.*] What *is* Pierre's "Just Society"?

FANON: *Trudeau au poteau!* Pierre to the gallows!
 Trudeau au poteau! Pierre to the gallows!

TRUDEAU:
  The Liberal Party programme is regional Realism, real Regionalism, Romantic Rationalism, rational Romanticism, Revolutionary Royalism, royalist Revolution, and representative Representation—

ROBERTSON: Freedom nation! Freedom nation!

FANON: *Domination! Domination!*

MARGARET: Liberation! Liberation!

Disgruntled, Cixous exits, huffily escaping the escalating pandemonium.

CIXOUS: [*Offstage.*] Hallucination! Hallucination!

FANON: *Annihilation! Annihilation!*

TRUDEAU: Go dream tonight, vote tomorrow.
  Tomorrow, vote for tomorrow!

MARGARET: Imagination takes command!

ROBERTSON: Liberty! Poverty is banned!

Trudeau leaves to the sound of rapturous cheers, applause, and boos. Margaret joins him as he exits. Fanon throws a stone at the podium.

ROBERTSON: Liberty! Peace! Equality!

FANON: Treachery! Treason! Treachery!

Robertson and Fanon face off against each other.

ROBERTSON: Participatory Democracy!

FANON: Chicanery! *Cochonnerie!*

The wash of helicopter takeoff drowns out the slogans.

Scene vi: Ottawa, Ontario, Autumn 1968

In the lobby of the House of Commons, Red-Light-District light, red and purple, bathes the scene. Margaret, in a white smock, holding roses, awaits Trudeau's arrival. Cixous and Robertson look on.

CIXOUS: Robertson, since his election,
　　Trudeau's buttoned-down, not much fun.

ROBERTSON: Simone, viewed up close, our debuted prime minister's
　　A *piñata* dangled before you punch-drunk reporters.

CIXOUS: He vroomed up to the Governor-General's residence—
　　In a Mercedes convertible and Manitoban buckskins.

ROBERTSON: Mobbed by miniskirts, he can't think!
　　He dons the mystique of the Sphinx.

CIXOUS: Arrives Trudeau at Parliament today![19]
　　Look! Mounties teargas the rabble away!

ROBERTSON: Teargas afflicts the just and the unjust—
　　Liberals as well as Conservatives.[20]

CIXOUS: Who voted for these acrid showers?

---

19 Cf. Shakespeare, Julius Caesar, I.iii.36.
20 Cf. John Fitzgerald Kennedy, 1960 U.S. Presidential Campaign.

ROBERTSON: Just blaze his path with fiery flowers.

Trudeau bestrides pinched Ottawa
Like a colossus, a Caesar.[21]

Fanon casts aspersions from the margins.

FANON: [*Aside.*] He's as cancerous as Caesar:
In depth, he's so superficial.

ROBERTSON: He comes now to the Capitol.

CIXOUS: Mesmerizing charisma fades
To peep shows and circus charades.

FANON: [*Aside.*] Québec hates no one more than him:
He loves us like a wolf loves lamb.

Laurelled, Trudeau appears in a Roman toga, sporting a rose corsage, and sandals. Margaret follows him as he parades into the Commons. However, she disappears into shadow as the spotlight focuses on Trudeau alone, clenching a flower stem between his teeth.

CHORUS: Trudeau, Trudeau!
It's way past spring!
Trudeau, Trudeau!
Now you're our king.

Trudeau, Trudeau!
Trudeaumania!
Trudeau, Trudeau!
Uh-oh, Canada!

---

21 Cf. Shakespeare, Julius Caesar, I.ii.134–135.

ACT IV

Betrayal flies around us.
It haunts the air we breathe.
THULANI DAVIS, X

Scene i: Monte Carlo, Monaco, April 1969

At a café, Trudeau, 49, and Margaret, 21, sit in wicker chairs, hold hands, and kiss. Both wear dark sunglasses, but Margaret's are Jackie O-styled gargantuan. She wears pastel bellbottoms, sandals, bandana, and a halter-top. Trudeau sports a T-shirt, a lightweight, pink sweater (the arms tied loosely around his neck), shorts, and sandals. Tennis rackets roost beside the pair as they sip champagne. In the margins of their rose light, Cixous skulks, aiming a camera with a phallic telephoto lens. Music here hints at Bruno Nicolai's perfect "Autostrada per Los Angeles" (1969) or Piero Piccioni's "Camille 2000" (1970).

TRUDEAU: [*Sipping.*] Relaxing in Monte Carlo,
  One drinks Monte Carlo *vino*—
  Champagne cocktails, plush, radiant,
  Liquid light, chilled, magnificent.

MARGARET: [*Lifting her sunglasses.*]
  When will we do it, Pierre? I'm crazy
  With waiting, with haunting, hazy,
  Shady cafés, as if we were
  Two soap-opera adulterers.
  When will we exchange rings, Pierre? When?

TRUDEAU: [*Sighing.*] Well, before the next election.

MARGARET: It's April 1969!

Am I to be a concubine—
As hidden as a mistress, hushed and banned,
While you frolic with Barbra Streisand?

TRUDEAU: Twelve months I've been prime minister!
A dozen months! Only one year!

MARGARET: Still, you have all the public fun!
  I'm the nameless—and nunnish—one:
  Anonymous, incognito—
  Your gal here in Monte Carlo!

Trudeau lifts his sunglasses, rises, and embraces Margaret.

TRUDEAU: *Fille* of slim limbs and *douce,* sigh-eyes,
  Sex can't surpass philosophies.

  When you have everything,
  Pretend you have nothing.

MARGARET: I don't need—right now—to pretend!
  Are you my love—or just a friend?

TRUDEAU: If you read Plato, you will know
  This world vaunts illusion.

MARGARET: Trudeau!
  Why can't I live *la vie en rose,*
  La dolce vita, dulcet, rose,
  Not stay cooped up in Ottawa,
  Cramming for French like corporate law,
  Exploring a nun's sterile life,
  Taking exams to be your wife?!

TRUDEAU: Being Prime Minister, I must clench
  A "wench" who charms *Anglais* and French.

MARGARET: [*Slyly.*] I know French … Do you know Dylan?

TRUDEAU: Dylan Thomas?

MARGARET: Nope! Bob Dylan!

TRUDEAU: [*Scornfully.*] Is he some revolutionary?

MARGARET: [*Laughing.*] As a folk-song poet—*very*!
    Sometimes you are *so* out of touch!

TRUDEAU: But still I boast a tender touch …
    Let's delay dawn by sleeping slow.

MARGARET: Feel sunlight warm up Monaco.

TRUDEAU: Let kisses quiet us to sleep.

MARGARET: If Sir Prime Minister can keep
        His promises,
                He keeps kisses!

Trudeau gets close and smells Margaret's perfume.

TRUDEAU: Your show-off scent attracts—like blondes
    As gala as sugar …

MARGARET: *Diamonds!*
    A gal must splurge to dress up innocence …

TRUDEAU: Virtue is jewellery—your gemmed essence.

MARGARET: [*Aside.*] Chrome, then silver, platinum, then diamonds,
    Scales conjugal progress.
    It's dull hell to regress!
    So, dude, hurry up: Legalize our bonds!

The lovers kiss. Cixous emerges from the shadows. A flashbulb bursts.

CIXOUS: Monsieur Trudeau—
 Please, *une photo!*

Both Trudeau and Margaret lower their sunglasses.

DUET: We'll keep kisses.

TRUDEAU: Mysterious!

Margaret raises her sunglasses and kisses Trudeau on the cheek while Cixous snaps another shot.

MARGARET: Photo-lustrous!

Lights down.

Scene ii: Ottawa, Ontario, April 1970

In the lobby of the House of Commons, brothel light saturates Gothic columns and gargoyles. Trudeau, 50, poses in a karate outfit, boasting a rose, while Cixous, in a pantsuit, with a camera and tape recorder, interviews him. Robertson stands outside the scene, which is 'boxed' or framed as if it were a giant television screen. He fiddles with giant knobs, as if trying to fix the picture.

ROBERTSON: [*Aside.*] An empty mirror,
 A naked emp'ror,
 A hackneyed athlete,
 An acne'd aesthete,
 An old news story,
 He's rusted glory:

A yesterday craze
In a purple haze!

CIXOUS: It's April 1970.
    Years pile up even as they flee.
    Mr. Prime Minister,
    Now in office two year,
    How do you gauge your government?

TRUDEAU: Simone Cixous, I've nothing to repent.

    Th'opposition's paid to protest—
    Crazed as vipers in a hornet nest.
    Donkeys, monkeys, flunkeys, and drabs—
    Circus of curses crapped by crabs—
    The "House of Comics" lacks all sense,
    C'est un bordel, a sty, of pretense.
    Its inmates squabble, squawk, and cry.
    (I am each member's chief bull's eye.)
    Rats backbite with crocodile smiles,
    Orate poster-and-slogan styles.

    Parliament howls, that wilderness—
    Kennel to foxes, jackals, and bitches …

    Tory brats, dainty socialists—
    Nattereri, Serrasalmus—[22]

    These baboon buffoons croon for Scotch:
    They act like they're in a pub, not Parliament.

CIXOUS: So you have become cynical?

TRUDEAU: Not in the least, just clinical:

---

22 A voracious class of piranha.

A prince must never degrade facts—
If his dreams would achieve uplift.

CIXOUS: Economists now want you axed:
They count you a "total spendthrift."

TRUDEAU: A good prince spends, a bad one steals:
Why should the rich rage that the poor eat meals?

CIXOUS: Aren't you exhausted by all the attacks?

TRUDEAU: I'm comfy in battle fatigues—*and* in slacks.

[*Aside, sniffing rose.*] I wear a rose on my lapel
To fend off the crowd's vicious smell.

CIXOUS: You appall Parliament, the press.
Now voters like you less and less.

TRUDEAU: Bankers' cash flows as ink in pens,
Turning newspapers into cannons.

Opinion-framers gang, complain,
Drool sleazy, sappy paeans to pain.

Journalists turn facts into jazz—
Their "truth" is never what truth was.

They love gutters and hate all curbs:
They rely on lies; I trust verbs.

CIXOUS: Critics clamour you're a "glamour puss."

TRUDEAU: I call them rank cancers of the ass!

[*Aside.*] I remain the agile target—
Adept at leap and pirouette.

CIXOUS: Are you a "philosopher-king"?

TRUDEAU: I like Sun Tzu, not the *I Ching*.[23]

CIXOUS: Thousands dream an independent Québec:
   What is your riposte to René Lévesque?

TRUDEAU: His Parti Québécois preaches suicide *amical*:
   Its schemes are practical jokes impractical.

   [*Aside.*] Riff-raff fall for flim-flam because
   Satan parades as Santa Claus.

CIXOUS: To air the Aboriginal Question,
   Seek you to "bleach" each "Indian"?

TRUDEAU: Let them pitch tents in society, not wax museums,
   Run corporations, not anthropology symposiums.

CIXOUS: But First Nations people say
   You "old-school white boys" think this way.
   Your policy urges them to rebel.

TRUDEAU: [*Shrugging.*] *Oui*, well, well, well …

CIXOUS: *Maintenant, on doit discuter* bilingualism:
   Is your programme "social Romanticism"?

TRUDEAU: I'm not trying to puff French down English throats!
   I'm not dying to stuff French down Anglo throats!

CIXOUS: Are any of your critics right?

TRUDEAU: Most of them are right-wingers, quite.

---

23 Sun Tzu is also Sun Zi; *I Ching* is also *Yi Jing*.

CIXOUS: Are you a fool—a Bay Street tool?

TRUDEAU: My sole luxury sums a swimming pool,
    Private. But Chairman Mao has one.
    Even prime ministers gotta have fun.

Trudeau bends and kisses Cixous on both cheeks. He exits. Cixous speaks into her microphone.

CIXOUS: An expert spirit (no slight style),
    Yet unfulfilling, like a smile—
    And manipulative as an octopus,
    But, like a tarantula, tenacious—
    This chameleon
    Masks a stealthy scorpion.

Robertson 'turns off' the 'set', plundging it into darkness. He is spotlit.

ROBERTSON: [*Aside.*] A two-faced speaker,
    A sideways leader,
    A funky Nero,
    A black-hole zero,
    A *kamikaze*
    For *paparazzi*,
    His politic craft
    Plies Superfly / Shaft.

Lights down.

Scene iii: Havana, Cuba, April 1970

*In a study, Fanon, in cut-off jeans, scruffy beard, dark sunglasses,
and a faded, khaki shirt, takes rum and cigars with Neruda, who is
wearing fatigues.*

FANON: A plaza intellectual—
  Well-versed in rehearsed reversal—
  A carnation politician—
  Carnal—

NERUDA: A polite mortician …
  A Caesar of party machines,
  Like a show horse, he sulks and preens.
  He's bilingual with double-talk—
  This snazzy, jazzy Jabberwock.[24]
  This April 19-7-0,
  Will Québécois draw-quarter Trudeau?

  [*Aside.*] I never trusted your Trudeau,
  Your flowery, Québécois beau.

FANON: Québec's enemy is Trudeau—
  King of crimes, tops in wrong and woe.

  A bullshit Machiavelli:
  Soft soap mixed with royal jelly.

  He's as shallow as a coffin,
  But just as polished, if not as often.

NERUDA: Fanon, workers lust for glamour.
  (Glamour is a kind of *amour*.)
  Thirsty for champagne, they'll drink piss.

---

24 A whiffling, burbling, fire-eyed creature, given to biting and clawing. It ends up
    beheaded in Humpty Dumpty's poem, "Jabberwocky," in Lewis Carroll's *Through the
    Looking Glass* (1871).

FANON: True Québécois trounce capitalists!
Le Front de Libération du Québec
Will plant two feet on every banker's neck!

NERUDA: Remember what Mao and Castro
Calculated, and since proved so:
"Political power flows and runs
Out of the barrels of our guns."

FANON: Traitors must fall! Trudeau must die!
That vampire apes a butterfly.

NERUDA: Everyone chats of liberty:
First, smash chains—to smash slavery!

Neruda hands Fanon his gun. Fanon hoists a drink in his other hand.

FANON: *¡Viva Cuba y el pueblo cubano!*

NERUDA: [*Saluting.*] *¡Viva la amistad cubana-canadiense!*

Scene iv: Ottawa, Ontario, October 1970

Sirens, explosions, and gunfire. Trudeau runs onstage in a Nehru jacket, cape, rose corsage, and helmet. He holds a machine gun. (He resembles Salvador Allende.) Behind him is a giant Canadian flag, but it is only partially visible because Trudeau is spotlighted. He sits in a wicker chair (mimicking a famous photo of Huey P. Newton). With a phone in one hand and the gun in the other, he shouts orders into the receiver.

TRUDEAU: The *Front de Libération du Québec*
Has taken hostages. I'll strike back!

Those bandits who assault democracy,
Now, this October 1970,
Will be smashed by any means necessary!

To hell with metaphysics!

(If Hamlet had had the icy, steely nerve of Macbeth—
In Hamlet, only two-faced Claudius would've faced red death.)

Smart governors swift eradicate
Aspiring assassins of the State.

*Spotlight up on Fanon, who speaks with his fist thrust high. He
stands before a Québec flag, but one featuring socialist-scarlet
fleur-de-lys. He holds a gun.*

FANON: As draconian as Dracula,
 Trudeau's a tyrant tarantula,
 But looks and acts an acne-pocked reptile—
 Cold-blooded, slithering, and spewing bile.

 Trudeau, true patriots each earn a statue.
 But traitors go to graves, and so will you.

Spotlight on Trudeau.

TRUDEAU: This mob is beasts, not men: This gang
 Swipes, at *nos citoyens*, claw and fang.
 I'll not let rebels wield their hooks,
 Rend our law and history books!

 My rightful might ignites from votes:
 No thugs usurp my thunderbolts!
 "Political power flows and runs
 Out of the barrels of my guns."

Spotlight now on Cixous, in trench coat and boots, holding up a microphone and looking toward Trudeau. Darkness separates the pair.

CIXOUS: These October nights, police shoot,
    Splash through doors and windows, then loot
    Homes, apartments, strip-searching books,
    Cuffing anyone with strange looks.

    How far will you go, Monsieur Trudeau?
    Monsieur Trudeau, how far will you go?

Spotlight on Trudeau.

TRUDEAU: Facing these villains, don't hold back:
    Pacify them by sneak attack.
    Crush—or gash—their veins jugular,
    But smile, appear avuncular.

    Blitzkrieg like Mao and Genghis Khan,
    Manoeuvre like crack Napoleon,
    Break skulls as if at Austerlitz,
    Fight like Castro at the Bay of Pigs.

Spotlight on Fanon.

FANON: Mao commands us to snatch up swords,
    Cut down landlords, and stab warlords.
    "Political power flows and runs
    Out of the barrels of our guns."

Spotlight on Cixous.

CIXOUS: Trudeau's sheer blood and iron these days:
    He chafes to whip his enemies.
    It's not enough, no, to jail each suspect:
    He must rectify, purify, correct!

He takes a jet to Ottawa.
He takes a whip to each outlaw.

He sees October through a gun-sight:
Halloween rattles us every night.

Spotlight on Trudeau. He shakes his fist.

TRUDEAU: Since terrorists lynched Pierre Laporte,
  Their manifestos at once abort.

  (How could Québec *Marxists* murder
  Québec's Minister of *Labour*?)

  I'll not quake under terror's awe,
  But reinforce the force of law,
  Chasten *Beretta*-and-beret
  Bandits, collapse their cabaret!

Spotlight on Cixous.

CIXOUS: In the gun-hushed, tank-trimmed Commons,
  Trudeau softens, with suave accents,
  The guttural blows of gloved fists
  Against free speech and liberties.

  How far will you go, Monsieur Trudeau?
  Monsieur Trudeau, how far will you go?

Spotlight on Trudeau.

TRUDEAU: Reporters, when will you stop
        scheming up nightmares from ink and Scotch?
  Whatever I defend, whether black or white,
        not one of you feels I'm ever right.
  Damn you! I'll grind these gangsters down alone:
        I'll confound what you condone.

Spotlight on Fanon. Sound of sirens.

FANON: I hear sirens! Is it the cops?
        Sirens wailing. Is it the cops?
  The front door's cracking, splintering!
        Catch skull-faced coppers entering?
  I know they mean to cause me harm!
        Who's there? *Firemen!* False alarm!

Spotlight on Cixous.

CIXOUS: How far will you go, Monsieur Trudeau?
  Monsieur Trudeau, how far will you go?

Spotlight on Trudeau. He struts, exaggerating his rage.

TRUDEAU: Just watch me! Just watch me!
  I'll bulletproof democracy!

  Rough up ruffians; bash these brutes:
  Flay their bones for drumsticks and flutes.

  Knife-fine, knife-coldly, knack their throats:
  Strike with the force of lightning bolts!

  Plunge thugs in shit! Drown em in piss!
  Let their vile blood blush their faces!

Spotlight on Fanon.

FANON: It's lousy Laporte got strangled:
  But freedom ain't got by angels!

  Yet Molotov cocktails quick boomerang:
  The boulevards bristle with troops and tanks.

I'll commence my quittance in Cuba:
Salut, Québec! ¡Hola la Habana!

Spotlight down. Chop of helicopter departing. Spotlight on Trudeau.

TRUDEAU: Butchers who strove hard to blackmail
    Our State now taste exile and jail.
    "Political power flows and runs
    Out of the barrels of my guns."

Spotlight on Cixous.

CIXOUS: How can men fire guns at others?
    In cloud-fog, aren't all men brothers?
    Who is whipping whom? Why? What for?
    In history's fog and fog of war?

Lights down.

Scene v: Ottawa, Ontario, Christmas 1972

Margaret, 24, appears in a white caftan, with a swaddled babe in her arms. During her first chorus and verse, sparkling confetti baptizes the scene.

MARGARET: The snow over Ottawa is falling stars
    This Christmas Day of our happiness.
    To Pierre and me, this boy-child appears—
    On a day famous for miracles.

    In Tahiti, I fell in love.
    It surprised me—like a chess-game move.

Last year, 1971,
We married, shocking everyone—
Like two stars on television ...

I'm young; Pierre's decades older:
I grow wise, while he grows colder.
I'm his wife, and now a mother,
Sunned by his star-power, his *remir*.[25]
But Canada is his real lover.

In our household, Pierre's glamorous,
Always vogueing for cameras.
He seeks applause, obedience.
I give him only love, but love
Merely bores our historians.

Pierre's duty makes him disappear
So much from our home, I appear
A widow—quite bereft of love.
It isn't fair. It isn't fair!
In Tahiti, I fell in love.

This Christmas Day of our happiness,
To Pierre and me, this boy-child appears.
On this day famous for miracles,
The snow over Ottawa is falling stars.

Trudeau, in a lawyer robe and carrying a briefcase, enters.
Margaret reaches out one arm to embrace him. But he points at
his briefcase, shrugs, and pirouettes away.

MARGARET: The snow over Ottawa is falling stars.

---

25 *Light*—in classical Provençal.

ACT V

Start a Long March on new highways.
GOODMAN

Scene i: New York City, USA, May 1979

Margaret, 31, in skirt, blouse (bra-less) and high heels, is dancing in a New York City disco. A mirror-ball light radiates the scene. Margaret sparkles, glitters; her underwear flashes.

MARGARET: In one swift decade, the Sixties vanished.
  I've borne three sons; but my heart's still famished.
  The world now tastes more sour than sweet.
  Why must love mark each wife's defeat?

  Once snazzy, Pierre aged nastier:
  At work a volcano; at home a glacier.
  No more a strenuous, avid lover—
  Just a penny-pinching "philosopher."

  My marriage morgued, now I'm solo,
  Liberated from overrated Trudeau,
  Chauvinist fart, dull as a pill,
  That fool chained to Parliament Hill.

  See, I could get no satisfaction.
  I had to get my satisfaction!

  Pierre's handlers manipulated me
  To hook votes for his Liberal Party.
  I broke free, smoked up with The Rolling Stones,
  Snagged a "black eye" once I "red-eyed" home.

But where was my satisfaction?
I had to get my satisfaction.

I shop now in Beverly Hills,
Feed my glamour to cannibals,
Cast my looks before the hoi polloi,
Dance pantyless through sleazy tabloids.

I had to get my satisfaction!
I could get no satisfaction!

Now I pursue photography,
Art that repays visibility.
I shoot the flush, the funky, the crazy.
I want to have Lou Rawls' baby!

Well, I could get no satisfaction!
So now I'm gettin satisfaction!

I remember everything Pierre taught
Me about loving—and about hate.
I'm gonna spite that autocrat
Who'd spout Plato in every spat.

Margaret withdraws a copy of Plato's Republic from her purse.

Let the "fame machine" maim fashion …
I've realized revenge—my passion.

Tonight, partly due to my defection,
Pierre's royally screwed this election.
Now I'm free to finally shine
This May 1979,
And can deposit Pierre's Plato
Where he best fits—like old *Play-Doh.*

Margaret tosses Plato in the trash.

To hell with Plato's Republic!
In America's republic,
I am finally who I am—
If not a star, at least a gem.

Lights down.

Scene ii: Gatineau, Québec, May 1980

*In the forest, Trudeau, 60, in a buckskin jacket and blue jeans,
paddles a canoe while giving an interview to Cixous, 45, wearing a
plaid skirt, cardigan, flat shoes, and socks.*

CIXOUS: Admit you have some lucky stars.
   Beaten last year, you've since won wars,
   Becoming once again P.M.,
   Triumphing in Québec's Referendum.
   Do you feel vindicated now?

TRUDEAU: Dear Simone, *dolce stil novo,*
   To cite Dante, "the sweet, new style"
   Is my programme: I yield an inch, but snatch a mile.

CIXOUS: Your ex gripes you sacrificed her for fame.

TRUDEAU: [*Shrugging.*] So what if history should know my name?

   Last year, when I crashed in defeat,
   I felt I'd been kicked in the teeth.
   Officed again, I must be expedient.
   Fame clasps the disobedient.

CIXOUS: Your agenda for the future?
   What's your next 'hurrah'—or encore?

TRUDEAU: Here I am, in my sixties,
　　But I announce the 1980s—
　　A new Canada, a new Canaan,
　　A gilt, sparkling Constitution,
　　Sunning a Just Society,
　　A rainbow of minorities—
　　Multicultural, bilingual, at peace.

　　Sagesse lights my bright policies.

CIXOUS: That is your generous theory.
　　It may collapse in history.

TRUDEAU: True: No *pays* can be constructed
　　To outlast deathless pyramids.
　　The only eternal policies
　　Are love and snow and death and ice.

CIXOUS: What is your opinion now of Parliament?

TRUDEAU: Most members are hardly Heaven-sent.

　　I've swum the Yangtze and the Bosphorus—
　　But Ottawa's tides are more treacherous.

CIXOUS: Is multiculturalism just your rainbow prism
　　To blinker or splinter Québec's nationalism?

TRUDEAU: There's no cultural purity.
　　Truth is there never was.
　　What we call humanity
　　Is a beautiful mess.

CIXOUS: This end of May 1980,
　　Lévesque shouts, *"Trudeau m'a fourré."*

TRUDEAU: He ejaculates vulgarity.
   He gambled, lost, and dares to cry!

   He acts like I peed on his snow,
   Bloodied his best white suit somehow.

CIXOUS: Separatists swear they got tricked.

TRUDEAU: Too bad. That's politics.

CIXOUS: Can you accommodate Québec?

TRUDEAU: You and I are housed in Québec,
   In evergreen-gorgeous Gatineau,
   Coupled closely in this canoe,
   Simone, I mean, 'Madelle'[26] Cixous:
   It's metaphor for Canada.

CIXOUS: [*Flustered.*] But … Pierre, we're not, we're not, no, ah—
   Lovers.

Trudeau beaches the canoe, then leans atop Cixous.

TRUDEAU: No, not lovers … Not yet …
   But you've followed me for decades,
   And I've always desired this date.

CIXOUS: We've not always seen eye-to-eye,
   You and I.

TRUDEAU: But, face-to-face, why
   Can't we consummate this passion?

CIXOUS: Remember: "The State has no place
   In the bedrooms of the nation."[27]

---

26 Ms. (Fr.)
27 Martin O'Malley coined this moral for a December 1967 *Globe & Mail* editorial.

TRUDEAU: But we're outdoors …

CIXOUS: You're out of place …

TRUDEAU: Am I, Simone? Am I? Our state
  Is a state of nature.

Trudeau peels off his jacket; Cixous undoes her cardigan. They kiss.

TRUDEAU: Checkmate!

Cixous pushes Trudeau away. She laughs.

CIXOUS: Well, where are we?

TRUDEAU: We're where we are.

CIXOUS: Pierre, just how far will you go?

TRUDEAU: Far.

They kiss and sink down into the canoe.

Scene iii: Montréal, Québec, 16 April 1984

Robertson sits at his piano in Biddles. He is interviewed by Cixous, T.V. camera in tow.

CIXOUS: Now that Trudeau's almost retired,
  Roscoe Robertson feels inspired
  To draft the man an opera:
  Is he a hero or horror?

  (This April 16, 1984,
  He's loathed especially in Alberta.)

ROBERTSON: I remember Pierre Elliott Trudeau,[28]
  That photogenic intellectual,
  Denouncing Duplessis in *Cité libre,*
  Crooning poems to Mao in October rain.
  I was caught in his reasoned, resigned reign—
  His classic curses, bilingual shrugs.
  (How his Cantonese befuddled pundits,
  How his Latin polished his puns and pranks!)
        Saw him in vivid 1968,
  Gesturing in confetti rain, flashbulb
  Lightning, in storming black-and-white footage
  Of his Caesarian coronation,
  Or in early, innocent spectacles—
  A people's genius in Bermuda shorts,
  Lecturing Asbestos strikers on laws
  To lasso Duplessis' cops, leash guns.
        Later, I watched his ordered troops parade
  Amid tumbling leaves and manifestos
  And cold October rain, in strange homage
  To Duplessis, and handcuff phantom fists
  That bristled, like pikes, prickling all Québec.
  I grinned at 'baaad', *Sesame Street* muppets
  Then watched helicopters stutter over
  Expo and whisk sad, puppet Québécois
  To Cuba, where Trudeau, years back, canoed.

        Now, despite Multiculturalism
  And the deft Charter of Rights and Freedoms,
  I fear he's a dandy, natty failure ...

CIXOUS: But few failures earn an opera ...

ROBERTSON: See Goodman: *Nixon in China.*

Lights down.

---

28 Cf. "War Measures." Quarry, 40.1–2, Winter/Spring 1991, p. 29.

Scene iv: Soweto, South Africa, April 1995

Trudeau, 75, stands at a podium with Nelson Mandela, 77, first president of a truly democratic South Africa. Both men wear dashikis.

MANDELA: In my jail cell, I read of you.
   Let us embrace, Monsieur Trudeau.

They embrace.

TRUDEAU: Mr. President Mandela,
   What joy, here, in South Africa,
   To greet our time's chief champion
   Of popular liberation.

MANDELA: Our comrade is Señor Castro,
   Champion of *socialismo,*
   And our time's great liberator.

TRUDEAU: No, sadly, just a dictator.

Castro, 69, wearing fatigues, enters.

CASTRO: [*To Trudeau*] In Cuba, Cubans dominate—
   Not capitalists or the United States.

Mandela takes both Trudeau and Castro by the arm.

MANDELA: This April 1995,
   Historians will mark in archives.

TRUDEAU: Out of office eleven year,
   Memory is now my treasure.

CASTRO: Why did you abandon your post, Pierre?
   Weren't you Canada's "Maximum Leader"?

TRUDEAU: I always thought ex-governors should wither away
          atop a mountain, polishing memories with wine,
    or gilding and refreshing Zen thoughts
          with dazzling, beatific wine,
    while rediscovering God
          between pine branches and the moon.

MANDELA: Such Romanticism can imprison.

CASTRO: Revisionism vitiates vision.

TRUDEAU: I walked in snow and saw no stars.
    I was a hero who'd outlived his wars.

CASTRO: The people's wars never end, Pierre.

MANDELA: For Cuba, total love I bear:
    South Africa's liberation
    Was triggered by the suave, Cuban
    Destruction of pale, *apartheid*
    Soldiers, their deaths—like suicide,
    Down at Cuito Cuanavale,
    Setting Namibia—then South Africa—free.

CASTRO: Comrade Mandela, we went there
    To crush a brother of Adolf Hitler.
    But, Pierre, you were upset by the
    Cuban army in Angola …

TRUDEAU: I was pissed off, Fidel, because
    You lied to me, lied without cause.

CASTRO: Liberation takes stern measures
    That contradict *bourgeois* pleasures.
    What's one lie to free a people?

TRUDEAU: In the shadow of the steeple,
    Statesmen slither and argue like devils.

CASTRO: We are instruments of evils
  To deliver Heaven on earth.

TRUDEAU: At any price?

CASTRO: What's Heaven worth?

MANDELA: I applaud your Charter of Rights and Freedoms,
  Trudeau, but look how far we slaves have come!

CASTRO: "Political power flows and runs
  Out of the barrels of our guns."

TRUDEAU: How can men fire guns at others?
  In cloud-fog, aren't all men brothers?

MANDELA: History isn't born, it's made.

CASTRO: Rulers walk in a lone parade.

TRUDEAU: We are old men now, soon to stand
  Within Eternity's remand
  And tout our triumphs, clear our crimes,
  Narrate our weighing of lopsided times,
  And how we balanced, how we fell,
  How we governed, how we rebelled.

MANDELA: Our children will guzzle the wine
  We have stored to age in cellars …

TRUDEAU: And they may—or may not—toast us,
  When that ripened wine wets their lips.

MANDELA: Our zenith is lush as autumn:
  Prosperous, we fall like each plum.

CASTRO: No governor waves off sorrow:
    If not now, it comes tomorrow.

Mandela pours wine into three glasses and looks out of a window.

MANDELA: Under wine-white stars,
        While night blackens, brown moths drum
    At this pane's gold light.

Mandela hands glasses to Trudeau and Castro. They toast him.

TRUDEAU: Gentlemen, we are old. I see
    Politics faint before Eternity.

Lights down.

Scene v: Montréal, Québec, October 2000

Trudeau, 80, in buckskin jacket and blue jeans, stands in the wooden chapel of Notre Dame Cathedral in Vieux-Montréal. His canoe rests beside a pew.

TRUDEAU: I shook my fist at fate,
    Then fate shook me.
    Fate took my youngest son
    But forsook me.

Enter Margaret, 52, in a black veil and black Mao suit. She looks at Trudeau.

MARGARET: I mistook you for my saviour,
    And you took everything.

TRUDEAU: Papa's early death turned me dour.

MARGARET: Too late, you're human, not a king.

Margaret exits.

TRUDEAU: I have merely been a traveller,
   All this lonely life, a wanderer,
   Searching always for my father,
   But I was also seeking Thee, Father.

   I could not find Thee, Father, until
   I lost my son. Two years ago,
   Before this year's millennial,
   My youngest boy, who was sheer gold,
   Vanished, fast, in an avalanche,
   All his beauty, my golden branch,
   Vanished neath ice.
   I'd've died twice—
   Gladly I'd've perished in his place,
   Switched my old bones for his sweet face,
   Then my grief would have turned to bliss.

   "Oh, God, why do you make us love
   Your gifts, then snatch them way from us,
   Before we've had mercy of death?"[29]
   Why did you take my young boy's breath,
   Leave me less a father with less a family?
   Rather, take my prizes and my trophies,
   And set them ablaze in a trice!
   Grant me my three sons, and my daughter,
   And I'd savour holy peace.

Trudeau steps into the canoe and kneels.

---

29 Cf. Shakespeare, Pericles, III.i.22-24.

At 20, I wanted revolution.
At 30, I wanted a doctorate.
At 40, I wanted attention.
At 50, I wanted love.
At 60, I wanted power.
At 70, I wanted influence.
Now 80, I would like forgiveness.

Death clarifies what good or ill
A man has done. "If I should tell
My history, it'll sound like lies,
Disdained in the analysis."[30]
But I have done, said, all I meant,
To graft beauty onto government,
Despite my faults, errors, and sins—
Of ignorance, of innocence.

But, I ask you, did I dream enough?
And I wonder, did I love enough?
Did I love my power all too much
And people not enough?

Are there new stars in the eternal sky?

Never prove indifferent to life!

Papa, mother, my children, I die,
Loving, with but love to satisfy.

My life's been a long, shining path,
A Long March down a shining path,
From birth and breath to aftermath.

---

30 Cf. Shakespeare, Pericles, V.i.108–110.

Trudeau paddles, under a spotlight, along a golden path, into a blackout. Lights gleam upon a coffin in the church. Robertson and Castro in black suits, and Cixous in a black dress, begin to sing while still offstage.

TRIO: His life's been a long, shining path,
    A Long March down a shining path,
    From birth and breath to aftermath.

Cixous, Robertson, and Castro slowly enter and stand about the coffin.

TRIO: "This leader? When comes another?"[31]
    "This choice spirit of the era—"[32]
    Bravura coloratura—
    Has no echo for his aura.
    Light dressed him: Bright was his grandeur.

    This Canada may pass away,
    But snow will still fall, rain still spray,
    His name be sung when dreamers sing.

Margaret enters, bends, and embraces the coffin.

MARGARET: I loved you—despite everything.
    I loved you—despite everything.

Robertson comforts Margaret and helps her to stand.

QUARTET: O Canada! May dreamers sing?

---

31 Cf. Shakespeare, Julius Caesar, III.ii.243.
32 Cf. Shakespeare, Julius Caesar, III.i.163.

L'ACTUALITÉ

*... I come of a
royal race myself*
MARQUIS

Unavoidably, this text mentions a galaxy of 'names' that fall within Trudeau's orbit. Nevertheless, the most famous occupy such a stratosphere of recognition that their omission here will be invisible. In all events, readers seeking more information about any of the personages presented in this drama need only consult their most treacherous biographers and most seditious historians.

Salvador Allende (1908–73) Chilean president assassinated during a U.S.-backed *coup d'état* against his elected Marxist government.

Josephine Baker (1906–75) African-American dancer, French *chanteuse*, Modernist art model, and *Résistance* heroine.

Lord Beaverbrook [Max Aitken] (1879–1964) Canadian tycoon and British politician.

Norman Bethune (1890–1939) The Ontario-born surgeon served as a doctor to Mao's 8th Route Army, eventually dying from septicemia.

Austin Clarke (1934–) A Barbadian-born, African-Canadian novelist.

John George Diefenbaker (1895–1979) 13th Prime Minister of Canada, 1957–63. His Bill of Rights (1960) anticipated Trudeau's Charter of Rights and Freedoms (1982).

Maurice Duplessis (1890–1959) Premier of Québec, 1936–39 and 1944–59.

Jeanne Duval Likely a Haitian Creole, she was a Parisian actress and mistress-muse to French Symbolist poet Charles Baudelaire (1821–67).

Chiang Kai-shek [*Jiang Jie-shi*] (1887–1975) Anti-Communist founder of Taiwan.

Pierre Laporte (1921–70) Québécois politician assassinated by *Front de Libération du Québec* goons.

Ferdinand Lasalle (1825–64) German socialist writer and journalist.

Irving Layton (1912–2006) A Romanian-born, Jewish-Canadian poet.

René Lévesque (1922–87) Québécois politician, founder, in 1968, of the Parti Québécois, and Premier of Québec, 1976–85.

Alice Munro (1931–) Anglo-Canadian short-story sculptor.

Huey P. Newton (1942–89) African-American co-founder of the (Maoist) Black Panther Party for Self-Defence in 1966.

Lou Rawls (1936–2006) African-American singer and screen actor.

Léo "Kid" Roy This popular, Montréal pugilist was Featherweight Champion of Canada in 1925.

RÉALITÉ

Beauty in art reminds one
what is worth while.

POUND

Trudeau: Long March, Shining Path (libretto by George Elliott Clarke, score by D.D. Jackson) is a recipient of Harbourfront Centre's inaugural *Fresh Ground new works* commissioning awards, initiated to stimulate collaborations between different art forms, disciplines and generations in creating new, multi-disciplinary artworks. In 2005, from 159 applications from across Canada, five projects were awarded $20,000 each toward completion. *Trudeau: Long March, Shining Path* will be presented as part of *New World Stage* at Harbourfront Centre, Toronto on 14 April 2007 in a performance directed by Graham Cozzubbo.

Trudeau: Long March / Shining Path debuted as a workshop performance at the Garden Room, K.C. Irving Environmental Science Centre, Acadia University, Wolfville, Nova Scotia, on 16 June 2006. The personnel were:

D.D. Jackson pianist
Janice Jackson soprano
 (*Cixous and Margaret*)
John Lindsay-Botten tenor
 (*Trudeau*)
Douglas Tranquada baritone
 (*Mao, Castro, and Fanon*)

It was also presented as a dramatic reading at the Helen Gardiner Phelan Playhouse, University of Toronto, Toronto, Ontario, on 26 August 2006. The personnel were:

Colin Taylor director
Jennifer Dowding apprentice
 stage manager
Philip Aiken *Neruda,*
 Robertson, Mandela
Marjorie Chan *Yu, Margaret*
Sonia Dhillon *Cixous*
Matthew Edison *Trudeau*
Von Flores *Mao, Kennedy,*
 Castro, Fanon

HANSARD

Everything has its beauty,
though not everyone can see it.
CONFUCIUS (KONG ZI)[33]

The sources for *Trudeau: Long March / Shining Path* were George Elliott Clarke, *Lush Dreams, Blue Exile: Fugitive Poems, 1978–1993* (1994); Leonard Cohen, "For E.J.P." (1964);[34] Thulani Davis, *X: The Life and Times of Malcolm X* (1992); Timothy Findley, *Famous Last Words* (1981); Ian Fleming, *You Only Live Twice* (1964); Kahlil Gibran, *The Prophet* (1923); Alice Goodman, *Nixon in China* (1987); Wayne Kostenbaum, *Jackie O* (1997); Nelson Mandela & Fidel Castro, *How Far We Slaves Have Come: South Africa and Cuba in Today's World* (1991); Mao Zedong, *Quotations from Chairman Mao Tsetung* (1972) and *Poems* (1976); Don Marquis, *archy and mehitabel* (1927, 1973); Max et Monique Nemni, *Trudeau: Fils du Québec, père du Canada* (2006); Richard Nixon, *Leaders* (1982); Otherwise Editions, *Trudeau Albums* (2000); Ezra Pound, *The Cantos* (1970), *Confucius* (1951), and "The Serious Artist" (1913);[35] Rainer Maria Rilke, *Duineser Elegien* (1922); Edmond Rostand, *Cyrano de Bergerac* (1897); Isaac Saney, "African Stalingrad: The Cuban Revolution, Internationalism, and the End of Apartheid" (2006);[36] William Shakespeare, *Julius Caesar* (1599), *Coriolanus* (1609), and *Pericles, Prince of Tyre* (1609); François-Xavier Simard, *Le Vrai visage de Pierre Elliott Trudeau* (2006); Pierre Elliott Trudeau, *Two Innocents in Red China* (with Jacques Hébert, 1968), "Notes for Remarks by Prime Minister Trudeau, Cienfuegos, Cuba, January 28, 1976" (1976),[37] and *Against the Current: Selected Writings, 1939–1996* (1996).

Many thanks to the Harbourfront Centre's "Fresh Ground" initiative for commissioning this libretto/opera in 2005; and to Fondation Pierre Elliott Trudeau Foundation, whose Fellowship Prize allowed me time and space to travel and to

33 See Jacques Hébert & Pierre Elliott Trudeau, *Two Innocents in Red China*, trans. I.M. Owen, Toronto: Oxford University Press, 1968, p. 34.

34 See Cohen's *Stranger Music: Selected Poems and Songs*, Toronto: McClelland and Stewart, 1993, pp. 80-81.

35 "The Serious Artist" appears in Ib.'s *Literary Essays*, ed. T.S. Eliot, New York: New Directions, 1935, pp. 41–57.

36 See *Latin American Perspectives*, 150, 33–5 (September 2006), pp. 81–117.

37 In March 2006, Dr. Keith Ellis, Professor Emeritus of Spanish at the University of Toronto, provided me with a typed transcript of these remarks.

support a workshop of the opera music; and to Dr. Sonia Labatt and Victoria University/University of Toronto for research and travel funds. I also thank Prof. Eugenia Sojka and the University of Silesia for sponsoring my Krakow sojourn. And I thank Prof. Linda Hutcheon of the University of Toronto for her support of the opera.

Trudeau: Long March / Shining Path was written in Turku/Abo, Finland; Edinburgh, Scotland; London, England; Monte Carlo, Monaco; Papeete, Tahiti; Moncton, Nouveau-Brunswick; Krakow, Poland; Halifax, Nova Scotia; Bucharest, Romania; Wolfville, Nova Scotia; Vichy, Biarritz, and Paris, France; Montréal, Québec; and Kingston, Jamaica; during 2005–07.

My libretto 'cabinet ministers' numbered Bettina Cenerelli, Flavia Cosma, Lindsay Dagger, Zetta Elliott, Keith Ellis, John Fraser, Sylvia Hamilton, Hao Li, Linda Hutcheon, DD Jackson, Ming Xie, Leilah Nadir, Elizabeth Peirce, Johanne Poirier, Simone Poirier-Bures, Robert Edison Sandiford, H. Nigel Thomas, and Paul Zemokhol. Special thanks to Richard Jackson for keeping DD and I informed about "new news" of Trudeau. Especial gratitude to Kate Kennedy and Andrew Steeves, of Gaspereau Press, for their exacting reading and beautiful suggestions. *Merci* to Geeta Paray-Clarke for interrogating (but not pardoning) my French. As 'prime minister' here, I assume full responsibility for all 'policy' fiascoes....

Thanks to the labour of editors Dr. Linda Burnett and Dr. Ric Knowles and of copy editor Rosemary Beattie-Clarke, the fourth draft of *Trudeau: Long March / Shining Path* ran in *Canadian Theatre Review* (No. 128, Fall 2006). (You are reading Draft VII.) Thanks to, respectively, Molly Peacock, Dae-Tong Huh, and Dr. Britta Olinder, excerpts of the libretto appeared in the *Literary Review of Canada* (14.10, December 2006), *Variety Crossing* (8th Edition, 2006), in English and in Mr. Huh's Korean translation, and in *Moderna Språk* (C.2, 2006), of Sweden.

COLOPHON

And beauty is not a need but an ecstasy.

GIBRAN

This book employs two digital revivals of types designed by the German calligrapher Hermann Zapf (b. 1918). The titles, footnotes and bold headings are set in PALATINO, designed in 1948 and cut in steel by August Rosenberger at the Stempel Foundry, Frankfurt. Adapted for virtually every successive typographic composition system, Palatino has become one of the most widely used typefaces, a surprising accolade for a type that was originally intended for hand-set display settings, not for continuous text. George Elliott Clarke reports that Palatino was used to set the English-language versions of Trudeau's *Two Innocents in Red China* (1968) and *Approaches to Politics* (1970). His admiration for these books led him to specify Palatino (as a kind of long-distance homage) in his poetry collection, *Lush Dreams, Blue Exile* (1994), and in his essays, *Odysseys Home: Mapping African-Canadian Literature* (2002). The body text of this book, however, is set in Palatino's lesser-known 'text' companion, ALDUS, designed by Zapf in 1953 for use on the Linotype composition system. Although Aldus is far better suited for continuous reading, it has never diminished Palatino's popularity as a text type. The difference in width and weight between these two types is obvious when they are compared at the same size, as they are below. Minor alterations were made to the fonts used in this book, including the introduction of a few new ligatures which were manufactured at Gaspereau Press. AS

Aldus Fuddle-Duddle & *Just Watch Me!* A Just Society?
Palatino Fuddle-Duddle & *Just Watch Me!* A Just Society?

VÉRITÉ

At once a necessary poet and an essential scholar,
George Elliott Clarke was born in 1960 in Windsor, Nova
Scotia, and grew up in working-class and 'Black' North
End Halifax. His debut poetry collection appeared in 1983.
Since then, he has published such prized titles as *Whylah
Falls* (1990), *Beatrice Chancy* (1999), *Execution Poems*
(2000), *Blue* (2001), *Québécité* (2003), and *Black* (2006).
His multiple laurels include the Governor-General's Award
for Poetry, the National Magazine Gold Award for Poetry,
the Archibald Lampman Award for Poetry, the Frontiera
Poesis Premiul (Romania), the Dartmouth Book Award for
Fiction, the Portia White Prize for Artistic Achievement,
the Bellagio (Italy) Center Fellowship, the Martin Luther
King Achievement Award, the Pierre Elliott Trudeau
Fellowship Prize, appointment to the Order of Nova Scotia,
and honorary doctorates from Dalhousie, New Brunswick,
Alberta, and Waterloo universities. A founder of the field
of African-Canadian literature, Clarke is the inaugural E.J.
Pratt Professor of Canadian Literature at the University of
Toronto, and owns land in Nova Scotia.

This book was typeset in Aldus & Palatino by Andrew Steeves & printed offset at Gaspereau Press under the direction of Gary Dunfield.

7 6 5 4 3 2 1

Library & Archives Canada Cataloguing in Publication

Clarke, George Elliott, 1960–
Trudeau : long march, shining path / George Elliott Clarke.
A poem.

ISBN 978-1-55447-037-2

1. Trudeau, Pierre Elliott, 1919–2000 — Poetry.   I. Title.
PS8555.L3748T78 2007   C811'.54   C2006-906946-8

GASPEREAU PRESS LIMITED
Gary Dunfield & Andrew Steeves · Printers & Publishers
47 Church Avenue, Kentville, Nova Scotia
Canada B4N 2M7   www.gaspereau.com